Young at Heart

Young at Heart

The Story of Johnny Kelley
Boston's Marathon Man

WRITTEN BY FREDERICK LEWIS
PHOTOS AND ESSAYS EDITED BY
RICHARD A. JOHNSON

Rounder Books

ROUNDER

Cambridge, Massachusetts

To Mary, Lizzy, Minna, Amy, Robert, and Bob —R.J.

To Nora —F.L.

In memory of Dr. Wayman Spence, Jerry & Jo Nason, Will Cloney, Les Pawson, and Jock Semple —F.L. and R.J.

DAILY RECORD
KELLEY NEAR RECORD
MARATHON VICTORY
S.S. America
60
BOSTON MARATHON
'91

TABLE OF CONTENTS

Acknowledgments 1

FOREWORD: Dr. Kenneth Cooper 3

Boston Marathon Map 6

CHAPTER 1: "Old Man Coin" 7

CHAPTER 2: "He Doesn't Even Look Tired" 13

CHAPTER 3: "Faugh-a-Ballough!" 23

ESSAY: Jerry Nason 29

CHAPTER 4: Heartbreak Hill Gets Its Name 33

CHAPTER 5: "Marathon Laufer" 47

ESSAY: Hal Higdon 60

CHAPTER 6: "What Time Is It?" 65

CHAPTER 7: "The Smartest Race I Ever Ran" 79

ESSAY: Jerry Nason 92

CHAPTER 8: "I'm Glad You Won, Stanley" 103

CHAPTER 9: Our Flag Was Still There 111

CHAPTER 10: Middle-Aged Marathoner 115

CHAPTER 11: Laura 131

ESSAY: John J. Kelley 137

CHAPTER 12: "I'd Rather Run Than Ride" 141

ESSAY: Amby Burfoot 153

CHAPTER 13: Landmark Years 165

ESSAY: James F. Fixx 171

CHAPTER 14: New Days, New Heroes 181

ESSAY: Jerry Nason 185

INTERVIEW: Bill Rodgers with Richard A. Johnson   188

CHAPTER 15: "I'm Gonna Make It!"   193

   ESSAY: Don Kardong   199

EPILOGUE   209

   CHART: Johnny Kelley's Boston Marathon Record   213

ILLUSTRATIONS

"CALLING ON JOHNNY KELLEY" Bob Coyne, *Boston Sunday Post*   22

"READY FOR THAT LONG GRIND" Bob Coyne, *Boston Post*   32

"OVER HILL AND DALE" Gene Mack, *Boston Globe*   66

"WHO'LL BE SECOND?" Bob Coyne, *Boston Post*   68

"JOHNNY KELLEY" Gene Mack, *Boston Post*   73

"JOHNNY KELLEY" Frank Lanning, *Providence Journal*   78

"BREAKING BRIDE'S MAID JINX" Gene Mack, *Boston Post*   90

ACKNOWLEDGMENTS

This book wouldn't have been possible without the support of many people. First and foremost are the late Johnny and Laura Kelley, who sat through many an interview and answered many phone calls as the manuscript was being prepared. The Kelley family, including Johnny's sisters Mary, Ruth, Margaret, Marion, and Katherine, all of whom shared memories of their big brother and family life on Palmer Street in Arlington, were tremendously helpful. Johnny's nephew Dan also supplied valuable genealogical information about the Kelley clan.

It helps to have an understanding family whether you're running marathons or writing about them, and Nora Lewis, Mary Johnson, and son Bobby were supportive and played the role of good sport to the hilt!

Among the many fellow runners who took part in this effort were the talented essayists who contributed original pieces to this book including: John J. "the Younger" Kelley, Amby Burfoot, and Hal Higdon. Also included are previously printed articles by Don Kardong, Jim Fixx, and Jerry Nason. Bill Rodgers, too, shared his insights on Johnny in the form of an interview.

We consulted many source materials for this project, not the least of which was the Marathon scrapbook of the late Jerry Nason. The "Boswell of Boston" was our constant spiritual companion, and we thank Jo Nason for having made this material available. The running chronicles written and published by Charley Robbins proved to be a godsend, and are contained in a gem of a volume covering five decades of running history in New England. Hal Higdon's piece on the Yonkers Marathon, which appeared in the May 1986 issue of *The Runner*, also proved indispensable.

Among the others who supported this effort were the ever-reliable Don Skwar, Sports Editor of the *Boston Globe*, the equally reliable and cooperative John Cronin of the *Boston Herald*, Guy Morse of the Boston Athletic Association, Jack Mahoney of John Hancock Life Insurance Company, former Boston Marathon Director Will Cloney, and 1948 Olympic marathoner Ted Vogel. We are also grateful to the late Leslie Pawson, Walter Young, Eve Dengis Bond, and North Medford Club legend Fred Brown.

We are deeply indebted to the man who had the vision and determination to launch this project, the late Dr. Wayman Spence. We are also grateful to his staff, including Margaret Leary, Terri Johnson, Jean Norwood, and Linda Filgo.

It is our sincere hope that this book conveys the inspiring message of Johnny's career while also shedding new light on the history of America's most honored footrace and marathoning in general. In a sport which has produced countless working-class heroes, John A. Kelley was certainly the most colorful and enduring.

FREDERICK LEWIS
RICHARD A. JOHNSON

January, 2005

FOREWORD

I'll never forget my first encounter with Johnny Kelley. We met on a Sunday morning in early February 1962 for a ten-mile training run arranged by our mutual friend, Dr. Warren Guild of Lexington, Massachusetts. At the time, I was a 30-year-old student at the Harvard School of Public Health making careful preparations to run the Boston Marathon.

I remember the three of us ran together at seven-minute pace for nearly nine miles. I couldn't help but be impressed by the fact that Johnny carried on an animated conversation the entire way, even though he was a good twenty-five years older than myself. With a mile to go in our run Johnny remarked to me, "Doc, if you don't mind, I'm going to jog on in." With that he accelerated to five-minute pace leaving us a good half-mile behind him at the finish. Needless to say I was impressed, very impressed! I was even more impressed two months later when, after having run a blistering 3:54 effort at Boston, I learned that Johnny had bested my time by nearly an hour!

Since that first training run, it has been my personal privilege to share the friendship of Johnny and his lovely wife Laura. In that time it has also been my professional privilege to witness and study the achievements of this remarkable athlete.

Johnny is a truly unique torchbearer for marathoning and aero-

bics in general. I can think of no other former Olympic or interna-
tional-class runner who has endured and continued to compete with
the dogged determination of my friend. He continues to set a marvelous example for athletes and non-athletes alike for conditioning,
training, and performance.

Since 1983 Johnny has made an annual visit to my clinic in
Dallas for a comprehensive fitness test, including a session on the
treadmill. The final results of these tests are contained in a series of
charts and computer printouts which, when analyzed, present a relatively complete portrait of an athlete's fitness. It is interesting to
note that while Johnny's test results place him in an extraordinary
category of fitness, they still don't completely explain his Boston
Marathon performances.

I feel Johnny has persisted because of many qualities we can't
quantify, namely his old Irish desire and his terrier-like tenacity. It is
a sure bet that whatever Johnny sets out to do, he'll do it—just tell
him he can't and see what happens! As his physician, I try to temper
that zeal to the extent that it's not dangerous. His commitment is
total, both to himself and his legions of fans.

Back in 1968 when I was putting the finishing touches on my first
book (*Aerobics*), I wanted to use Johnny's story as one of the many
first-hand accounts of aerobics athletes I included in the book. For
the most part these accounts were drawn from my friends and con-
tacts at Lackland Air Force Base where I was stationed. I thought
that Johnny would fit in perfectly and had already written up his
story when I contacted him for his permission.

Even Johnny can laugh today when he recalls that he flat out
refused to cooperate with me. I remember him saying that he had "to
do all the running and why should someone else get the money." I
tried to explain that this was my first book and that I'd be thrilled if
even my mother bought a copy. To this day Johnny remains the only
person, in my twenty-six years as an author, who has ever refused to
let me put his name in one of my books.

I can kid Johnny now about the fact that *Aerobics* has been trans-
lated into forty-one languages! I let him know that people across the
world would've learned about him, and to Johnny's credit he admits
he made a mistake.

Now at long last I am delighted that Johnny's story is to be told.

And while he was unwilling to be part of my book, it is my happy privilege to write the introduction to his book!

I trust you will find his story to be both enlightening and inspirational.

—KENNETH COOPER, M.D.

Dallas, Texas
December, 1991

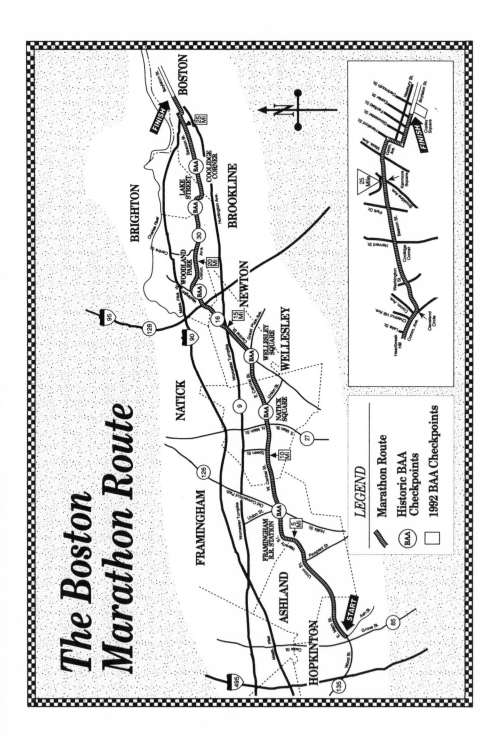

Chapter 1
"OLD MAY COIN"

"*R*unning is a way of life for me, just like brushing my teeth," says John A. Kelley, age 84. "If I don't run for a few days, I feel as if something's been stolen from me." Each morning around 5 A.M., this small but sturdy octogenarian awakes and rises from bed. While Laura, his wife of 34 years, sleeps a while longer, he heads down to the finished basement of his cedar-shingled home. "I go down and check the temperature outside, then I pick out what running clothes I'm gonna wear and change up. Then I go back upstairs and empty the dishwasher, set the table and fill the coffee pot. I'm limbering up, see?"

By 5:30, Johnny Kelley is out the door. Flashlight in hand, he is gone to greet another sunrise on Cape Cod. He walks a few hundred yards in the early darkness, then he trots a bit, then he begins to run. Johnny Kelley is no fair-weather jogger. Barring a blizzard, he is out there. He moves with the nimble stride of a man half his years, doggedly churning out the miles. "I look forward to my runs," he says. "I run alone. I don't like to wait for people." Sometimes he'll cut through the woods on a pine-scented path that leads to a nearby golf course. Other days he'll head for Sea Street Beach and run along the shoreline, or trace the deserted roads that wind through the village of East Dennis. "It's a great way to get acquainted with yourself," he explains. "I love it. I just go along and think the good thoughts, think about my life. The air is fresh and sweet. The other day at Nickerson

State Park, two deer ran out in front of me. And there's a fox I chase every once in a while."

Often, these hour-long jaunts conclude with a strenuous climb up Cedar Hill Road. Three steep inclines must be conquered before he is back to his cozy, ranch-style home, back to his beloved Laura. By 7:30, he has showered and dressed, prepared breakfast, and is reading the morning paper when Laura joins him.

It is a relatively small part of his day, this solitary hour or so of running, but running is the essence of Johnny Kelley's long life. He has been doing it for more than 70 years. He is living testimony that remaining physically active throughout one's life is the best antidote for aging. Johnny Kelley, you see, not only runs, he still runs marathons—the Boston Marathon to be precise, and he has been running it for 60 years! His love affair with this fabled footrace has made him nearly as well-known as the event itself.

Every April, on Patriots' Day in Massachusetts, the strongest and swiftest runners in the world journey to their mecca. But their day in the sun is fleeting. "Old Kel" is the true victor, the one the crowds adore. Generations of Greater Bostonians have grown up watching this plucky little man make his annual trip down Glory Road. They wait for him to pass by, they call out his name: "John-nee, John-nee!" Amid the deafening chants and applause, his blue-green eyes are fixed on the pavement before him. But sometimes they soften, and a tear or two escapes. He waves and smiles at the thousands of expectant faces and the ovation grows even louder. "It makes me cry," Johnny admits. "And a lot of them are crying, too!"

Johnny Kelley's amazing longevity sometimes threatens to diminish what he accomplished in his prime. He is an athlete of the highest order, a three-time Olympian and two-time winner at Boston. But Johnny's heyday was not without its disappointments. No one has experienced more intimately the myriad of emotions the marathon can stir in a runner. He finished second at Boston a heartbreaking seven times. "I was a big part of a lot of great battles at Boston," he says. "I'm just part of the furniture now. To me it's like Old Home Day. It seems I've spent a good part of my life running down Commonwealth Avenue."

"God's been good to me," Johnny says, passing his hand through wispy white hair. "I've caught a few bad breaks along the way, but

God likes me. And I like Him, too. Time marches on and here I am way up in my 80s. Jeepers. I want to run till I'm 100. I'll never stop," he declares. "People ask me about my philosophy of life all the time," he says with a shrug. "I just put one foot in front of the other and keep going."

Johnny Kelley has led a marathon life in more ways than one. He has known grief and glory, disappointment and delight. The simple, inspiring lesson all of us can learn from this sometimes feisty, always self-effacing champion, is that life's greatest victories go not to the fastest, but to those who endure.

In 1905, William J. Kelley of Boston, Massachusetts, was a very energetic man, always active, always in a hurry. He was working for Bigelow-Kennard, a Boston jewelry store when, on his lunch break, he stopped at the Old Corner Bookstore. There he met Bertha Kilburn, who was also browsing among the books. Quiet, patient, and artistic, Bertha had attended business school in Fitchburg, Massachusetts, and was working as a secretary for *Mercury* magazine. She was living at the YWCA and traveling home to the town of Lunenburg on weekends. Though she was born in Nebraska, her family was originally from New Hampshire. William Kelley soon became Bertha's one and only beau.

William's parents had emigrated from County Wexford in Ireland, arriving in Boston on April 10, 1870, aboard the *S.S. Marathon*, surely a lucky omen for William and Bertha's first child. John Adelbert Kelley was born in West Medford, Massachusetts, on September 6, 1907. "My mother and father, when they were keeping company before they got married, used to go watch the Marathon," Johnny says. "My mother said she never thought she'd have a son that would win it."

Early on, the Kelleys were poor. Johnny remembers trying to hide a hole in his shoe by lining it with cardboard and newspaper. "I was only five years old. My mother saw the bottom of my foot and it was all blood and dirt. She took me right into Boston by streetcar to see my father at work and told him, 'We've got to get this kid some shoes and take care of his feet.' " Bertha Kelley didn't know it then, but her son Johnny would one day become famous by wearing out shoes.

Bertha Kilburn Kelley loved music. She played the harp and the piano and was the organist at church. She instilled in all of her children a love for music and song. Some mornings, instead of going from room to room to wake her offspring, she would simply sit down at the piano and sing to them. "She was a little bit of a woman," Johnny says. "We all had piano lessons, but I didn't keep them up. I should have."

William Kelley was the quintessential Irish Catholic patriarch. If you didn't go to church on Sunday, you didn't go out at all. "He was strict," Johnny says, "but he'd cut off his arm for his children. He would. He gave me the best description of married life anybody ever gave me. He said, 'You'll have things in married life that'll just about break your heart. And you'll have things the next day that'll take you way up to the skies again.' And it's very true."

Struggling to support a brood that would eventually grow to ten—five boys and five girls (an eleventh child died in infancy), William Kelley left Bigelow-Kennard and moved his family from Charlestown to Medford. He became a mail carrier, a job that better suited his constant need to be outdoors and on the move, a trait Johnny certainly must have inherited. In fact, Johnny would walk the route with his father, helping deliver the mail.

In those days, the North Bennett Street Union Industrial School in Boston's North End ran a caddy camp in the White Mountains of New Hampshire. Though the Kelleys now lived in Medford, Emmett Kelley, a cousin, arranged for Johnny, and later his brothers Jim and Willie, to attend the camp, thus lightening Pa Kelleys load for a while. From age twelve to fifteen Johnny spent four splendid summers in the White Mountains as a caddy at Maplewood and Bethlehem.

Walking his father's mail route had helped prepare Johnny for his New Hampshire summers as a caddy. "I walked and walked and walked," he recalls. "We used to get seventy-five cents for eighteen holes. Sometimes we'd carry two sets of clubs at once. I only weighed about 95 pounds. The golf bags were bigger than I was but, looking back, that was my basic training. My legs were getting stronger and stronger."

But even in New Hampshire Johnny could not escape the playful jokes his younger brothers loved to play on him. Johnny's sister Mary remembers that one year Johnny realized he hadn't packed enough clothes to make it through the summer and wrote home asking for more to be sent. "My brothers put together a package that consisted of a brassiere and an old corset, Pa's old painting trousers and paint bucket, and some dumbbells Johnny used to exercise with. They sent it C.O.D.," Mary recalls. "When Johnny paid the charges and opened up the box, he was furious. He wrote and told Ma, and she sent him what he needed. Johnny didn't think it was very funny at the time."

Around this time, Johnny's siblings tagged him with a nickname they continued to tease him with throughout his life. "Johnny'd go around picking up rags and bottles and sell them to Sam Wax, the ragman," remembers Mary. "He always seemed to have a little change in his pocket—pennies and dimes and nickels. My other brothers would always try to borrow some. One day brother Jimmy said, 'Gee, you're Old Man Coin.' And it stuck."

"Old Man Coin" loved to play sports. Too small for football and too smart to risk a broken nose in the boxing ring, Johnny turned to baseball, a game he still loves. "We had a uniform team. We had evening games and we used to draw large crowds. I played left field but I couldn't hit very well—so one day the ball was coming and I said, 'It's gonna break, it's gonna break.' It almost broke my head. So they took me down to the brook and dumped my head in the brook, and that was about the end of my baseball career."

His batting average continued to dwindle, but Johnny soon got his first taste of athletic success. A field day was held at Playstead Park in West Medford. "We were playing a sandlot ballgame, but I got them to stop the game so I could run the race." Johnny entered the quarter-mile run and finished second. His prize? A baseball bat.

Chapter 2
"HE DOESN'T EVEN LOOK TIRED"

In 1921, William Kelley said to his oldest son, "If you behave yourself I'll take you to the Marathon tomorrow." Johnny wasn't quite sure what a marathon was really all about yet, but he does remember playing World War I games by the Mystic River a few years earlier and coming across a week-old copy of the *Boston Globe* yellowed by the sun. The *Globe's* faded headlines proclaimed Carl Linder the winner of the 1919 Boston Marathon. A New England decathlon champion from Quincy, Linder won the 24 1/2-mile footrace after having been rejected for military service because of flat feet.

By the time William Kelley took 13-year-old Johnny to watch the race, the Boston Marathon had already become a New England tradition. First run in 1897, it started at Metcalfe's Mill in Ashland and finished in Boston, with one lap around the track at the Irvington Street Oval. Fifteen runners toed that first starting line. The following year, the race began on a railroad bridge in Ashland and finished on Exeter Street in front of the clubhouse of the exclusive Boston Athletic Association, founders of the race.

The first modern Olympiad had been held a year earlier in Athens. A large delegation from the affluent B.A.A., which had sponsored the United States team, attended. The B.A.A. members were so impressed by the efforts of winner Spiridon Louis, a Greek shepherd, that they decided to stage a similar event on U.S. soil. The

B.A.A. elected to run their marathon on April 19th—Patriots' Day in Massachusetts—a holiday that commemorates the midnight ride of Paul Revere and the Revolutionary War battles at Lexington and Concord in 1775.

Early on, the actual length of the Boston course varied. From the time of its inception until 1923, it measured about 24 1/2 miles. Not until '24 did the B.A.A. attempt to conform to the international standard of 26 miles, 385 yards, a peculiar distance established in London at the 1908 Olympiad. Because of sickness, the royal family was unable to attend the proposed start of the marathon. Olympic officials overcame this dilemma by bringing the start to Wmdsor Castle, thus extending the course by one mile, 385 yards.

On Patriots' Day of 1921, William Kelley and his oldest son traveled by streetcar to Commonwealth Avenue, near the Marathon finish line. The crowds, anticipating the approach of the winner, were already tightly bunched, making it difficult for the Kelleys to see. "A big Irish policeman saw me and held the rope up so I could get a better look," Johnny remembers. Standing in front of the crowd-control ropes, Johnny had a perfect view of the victor, Frank Zuna, flying toward the finish in record time. Zuna was a powerfully built plumber, a working-class athlete, as were all the early marathoners. He had arrived from Newark, New Jersey, a bit disheveled, wearing his running clothes under his rumpled suit and with a racing shoe protruding from each of his jacket pockets. But the Frank Zuna that young Johnny Kelley saw come striding down Commonwealth Avenue in his white shirt and shorts did not look unkempt or seedy at all.

"I remember my father saying, 'He doesn't even look tired, look at him.'" But Johnny was already looking, entranced by the scene of Zuna savoring his victory. "I can still see the look on his face today," Johnny says.

It wasn't until he attended Medford High School in 1923 that Johnny experienced his first true taste of distance running. Medford had its own indoor track and Johnny was fascinated by it. "It was just a little saucer-shaped thing. If you weren't careful you could get real dizzy and fall right off it." Johnny ran the 600- and 1000-yard events.

But his stay at Medford High was short. "We moved across the river to Arlington, where my father bought a ten-room house on

Palmer Street." At first the neighbors weren't thrilled to have a family with ten children move in. But William Kelley was very strict and his children were well-behaved. Soon the Kelley kids were favorites with their new neighbors, running errands for them and taking care of their yards.

At Arlington High, Johnny ran cross-country and the mile and two mile. Under Arlington's longtime coach, Dr. William T. McCarthy, Johnny began to excel. At last he had found a sport he could call his own, though for a time he shared the family spotlight with brother Jimmy. "Jimmy was a better runner than I was, but he gave it up after high school." Johnny's high school best for the mile, around 4:40, remains his personal record. His accomplishments on the track and as captain of the cross-country team made him one of the four or five best-known athletes in the school. But Johnny wasn't allowed to bask in his new-found popularity. As the oldest of ten children, he was expected to go to work.

He got a job pumping Tydol gasoline and greasing cars at Leonard Collins' service station across from the high school. "I'd get out of school around one o'clock and work 'til about three. Then I'd go over to the field for practice. Sometimes I'd go back after practice and work from six to nine. My sisters would bring my supper down to me and I'd do my homework at the desk inside the station. I got 35 cents an hour. Gas was 15 cents a gallon."

Upon graduating in 1927, Johnny tried to find steady work, but the Great Depression was looming. With time on his hands, he began running in road races. Massachusetts was then the nation's road running hotbed. For decades, most of America's finest long distance runners came from the New England region. Many of the national distance championships were held in the area simply because this was where the best runners were. At a small local event in Rockland, Johnny ran his first five-mile race and came in second, winning his first loving cup. "We finished on Liberty Field at second base—that was the finish line. 1927—geez that's a long time ago." He didn't know it then, but he had run right past the house where his first wife, Mary, was born.

Many of the ten milers Johnny ran were handicap races: "In a handicap race the novice runners were given a head start, while the more experienced men were given a time handicap—in my case I would always start at the scratch line. The biggest handicap anyone could usually get was five minutes, but at some races they'd give more. There'd always be a prize for the first finisher, but they'd also give a time prize to the fastest overall. They were the most fun. You couldn't do anything like that now with the thousands of runners that show up at races today. But the handicappers would usually do a terrific job in judging the talent. They'd get 10 cents a man."

For a few years, Johnny Kelley was a member of the North Medford Club, today one of the oldest running clubs in New England. Dues were 25 cents a month. "Originally, North Medford had club football and baseball teams," Johnny says. "There were about twenty or so of us runners they took in under their wing—Fred Brown, Bill Molloy, and many others. But then the runners started getting an awful lot of publicity and that caused some friction. So the runners broke away and formed their own club." One of Johnny's teammates with the North Medford Club was "Smilin' Jimmy" Henigan, a popular, stoop-shouldered little runner with a seemingly perpetual grin. Often, Jimmy wasn't really smiling at all. The torture of marathoning caused his grimace to look like a grin. "Jimmy Henigan was a little gentleman. He was one of my idols when I was coming up."

James Henigan's racing career was similar to Johnny's in accomplishment and frustration. Both would become three-time Olympians, Henigan in '24, '28 and '32. Both excelled at distances between ten and twenty miles, but had trouble with stamina in the latter stages of marathons. Despite a long list of achievements, Henigan's ambition was to win the Boston Marathon. He ran the race seven times before he even managed to reach the finish. Several times during that string he had fought for the lead for twenty miles, only to fatigue and fold. After another courageous attempt in 1927, Henigan swore he'd never return. But a year later he did, completing the course for the first time, placing second.

After failing to finish the next two years, Jimmy Henigan achieved his dream. In 1931, four days before his 39th birthday, he made it to the finish on Exeter Street ahead of the field. He had to alternately walk and run the last three miles because of badly blistered feet, but "Smilin' Jimmy" made it, and the crowds cheered wildly. In 1932 he would again finish second. "He was a big help to me, an inspiration," Johnny says of Henigan. "One of the finest runners I've ever known."

In 1928 Johnny Kelley, 5 foot 6, 121 pounds, attempted his first marathon. "It was on St. Patrick's Day down in Rhode Island. Pawtucket to Woonsocket and return. I was up with the leaders, but on the way back I faded badly. I could see the city of Pawtucket off in the distance, but I never could seem to get anywhere near it; it was like a mirage. I finished seventeenth. I ran three hours and seventeen minutes."

A month later Johnny decided to take his first crack at Boston, which was an Olympic trial that year. Travel bag in hand, he caught a streetcar to North Station. In the '20s, the B.A.A. chartered a pair of train cars that carried the runners, race officials, and club members from North Station to Framingham. Buses transported the party the rest of the way to Hopkinton. When the stock market crashed the following year, many B.A.A. members lost their fortunes and this extravagant practice was ended.

The course had been remeasured several times by 1928, and now started in the village of Hopkinton instead of Ashland. Among the record field of 254 starters who gathered in the bucolic hamlet were the legendary Clarence DeMar, a seven-time winner at Boston, and Joie Ray, a world-class miler attempting his first marathon. Johnny endured for twenty-two miles, through Ashland and Framingham, Natick, Wellesley, and Newton. Finally, at Cleveland Circle in Brookline, he slowed to a weary walk.

"It was too soon to run another marathon. What did I know? With four miles to go I was walking along the road, and a man came over and touched me on the arm and said, 'C'mon young fella, I'll take you in if you want a ride.' It was a great temptation." Johnny took the ride the rest of the way to the B.A.A. clubhouse near the finish. "I always wished that I had the man's name so that I could have called him when I won Boston several years later."

Clarence DeMar won his sixth Boston that day, followed by Jimmy Henigan. Joie Ray, the miler, finished third, his feet so bloodied by blisters his shoes had to be cut from his feet. Incredibly, Ray's feet would heal well enough for him to win the next Olympic trial in New York a month later, making him a three-time Olympian in distances ranging from the 1500 meters to the marathon. He would go on to the Games in Amsterdam and finish fifth in the marathon. "He was from Illinois," Johnny says of Ray. "They used to call him the 'Kankakee Kid.' I used to idolize Joie Ray. I think he was the prettiest runner I ever saw in all my life."

Johnny Kelley would not attempt another Boston Marathon for four years, instead concentrating on five milers and the handicap races he loved. He wasn't winning any major races yet, just running for enjoyment. His parents weren't exactly supportive. Throughout much of his competitive career, runners were regarded as oddballs. The common cry around Patriots' Day was, "It must be spring; the saps are running again." Besides, a healthy young man like Johnny should have been out looking for work. "No, my parents were not supportive at the beginning of the running business at all, especially my mother. You see, my parents didn't understand," Johnny explains. "This was the Depression. Running was something to do. There were no jobs anyway. I worked here and I worked there, I worked for the town of Arlington for a while—there was nothing permanent, nothing steady. Running was fun. It helped kill time."

The blue-collar marathoners of the '30s and '40s ran three or four days a week, logging anywhere from thirty-five to sixty miles. Some did more, but most adhered to the conventional wisdom of the day that said too many more miles would either deaden you on race day or damage your heart. "I don't think I've ever run more than sixty miles a week in my life. Ever. Some of these runners today do twice that much. I ran on the watch, never on miles. If you said to go out and run fifteen or twenty miles it would scare me. But two hours or an hour—I've always trained that way."

Johnny was beginning to make his mark at the shorter races around New England but he realized that sooner or later he would have to return to the Marathon. "The Marathon was where you had to go to make a name for yourself so that's where I went. A win at Boston was the equivalent of winning two hundred other races. In 1932 I was still just a greenhorn. I put Vaseline all over my feet and wore heavy wool socks. I was with the leaders, Henigan and a few others, but at Wellesley—halfway—my feet were all blistered, all blood. So I stopped. And the next year, 1933, I had the flu. I never should have been in the race in the first place, but when you're young, you know, you know everything, so I ran it and finished in

37th place. My good friend Les Pawson won it that year."

In '33 Leslie S. Pawson was a mill weaver in Pawtucket, Rhode Island, but he ran with the smooth stride of a college track star. For years the marathon had been regarded as simply an endurance contest. Pawson contended that the race could be run much faster if more marathoners incorporated speed work into their training. Les put to use the skills he'd gained running track and shorter distances on the roads, and set the example. Fighting a vicious head wind that left his face, arms and legs badly windburned at the finish, he set a new course record and outdistanced Canada's Dave Komonen by nearly five and a half minutes, changing forever the way runners would approach the Boston Marathon. Were it not for the head wind, he might have slashed a few more minutes off the record. The triumph also helped Pawson move out of the Lorraine Mills and into a job as a park supervisor in Fairlawn, his Pawtucket neighborhood.

Leslie Pawson would win the Boston Marathon three times. The *Boston Globe* once said of him, "No runner is so respected by his contemporaries as Pawson for his intelligence, even temperament, mannerliness and competence as a runner."

Johnny Kelley and Leslie Pawson have known each other for more than sixty years. "He's a close friend," Johnny says. "He was the best man at my wedding when I married Laura. I couldn't think of a finer person to have stand up for me. He was a great runner, as good as I was—better in fact. He had an enormous kick at the finish. No matter what the distance. I never had that.

"One time many years ago they had a three-mile run in the Boston Garden, at the B.A.A. Games, and it was for marathon men only and all the college boys wanted to get in it. Les won it and they said it was the biggest kick-burst they ever saw in the Boston Garden. Les was so dizzy they had to help him off the track."

"John was a real scrappy runner," recalled Pawson. "He'd hang on all the time. Winning was very important to John. He wanted to win every race. He'd run himself so hard sometimes he'd get sick. But he always managed to finish. He'd come down to Rhode Island sometimes and we'd train together."

"Over the years, of all the runners I've ever known," Johnny says, "Les was the only one I enjoyed training with. I'm very fond of him. But when the gun was fired in a race it was every man for himself."

Johnny Kelley's affection for Leslie Pawson is genuine. Indeed, when Johnny talks about the glory days, he mentions Les Pawson's name repeatedly, in an unselfish effort to share the spotlight that these days shines only on him.

Pawson's victory marked the beginning of a new, more colorful era in the Boston Marathon's history. Pawson and Kelley would combine with a flashy French Canadian named Cote (pronounced Cotay) and a Narragansett Indian named Brown, to win the race eleven times in sixteen years. In many ways this was Boston's golden era, though there was little gold in it for these working-class amateurs who battled each other perennially.

1934 was Johnny Kelley's breakthrough year. A few years earlier, the North Medford Club had established a twenty-mile race that toured the towns of Somerville, Stoneham, Malden, and Medford. Held in March, it proved to be a popular tuneup for April's Marathon. Les Pawson had won the first two, but this third edition belonged to Johnny. It was a race he never expected to win because of the stellar competition. But after seven years of road racing, "I was like an apple on a tree getting riper and riper. My mother and father were there, which surprised me, but I happened to win it—the first big race I ever won. In the beginning they didn't know much about it, but from then on they were all for it. My brothers and sisters were all for it too."

For the first time, 27-year-old Johnny Kelley began to look toward the Boston marathon with confidence. Les Pawson was the defending champion, but the favorite in the '34 B.A.A. was Taavi "Dave" Komonen, a Finn who had emigrated to Canada and settled in the mining town of Sudbury, Ontario. Komonen had won both the Canadian and American marathon titles in '33. Before emigrating he had occasionally trained with his idol and countryman, Paavo Nurmi, the legendary middle-distance runner. A carpenter by trade, Komonen was also a cobbler. The shoes he raced in had homemade heels.

Bill Steiner of New York set the early pace, but Komonen took over halfway, just past the crowds of cheering women at Wellesley College. The only runner who went with him was young Johnny Kelley. "It was a cold, dark day," Johnny says. "I can remember Komonen kept looking at me as if to say, 'Who are you and what are you doing staying with me?' "

For eight miles the two bantam runners battled, Johnny's black hair soaked with sweat, Komonen's covered with a knotted handkerchief to avert any sun. Johnny forged a short lead several times, but Komonen would reclaim it quickly. Blisters began to hamper Johnny's stride. Passing the spires of Boston College on the last of the three Newton hills, Komonen yelled out, "Rata Auki!," Finnish for "Clear the way!" Komonen's 10-yard lead began to lengthen. It was 30 yards by Cleveland Circle, 300 by Coolidge Corner. Over the last five miles, Komonen outdistanced Johnny by nearly four minutes, finishing in 2:32:53. Johnny limped home in second place, hardly disappointed, in 2:36:50. He had broken through to the big time. Over the next twelve years he would play a leading role in virtually every Boston Marathon.

Chapter 3
"FAUGH-A-BALLOUGH!!"

$\mathcal{H}$aving proven to himself and to others that he could stay the course, Johnny began making plans for the 1935 B.A.A. One of the first things he did was seek some coaching advice. Frederick Faller, a watchmaker from West Roxbury, worked at Bigelow-Kennard, the same company Johnny's father William had worked for when he was courting Bertha Kilburn. Faller had been a 10,000-meter runner at the 1920 Olympics in Antwerp, Belgium and was an accomplished road runner. Past his prime, he had turned to coaching and had helped Les Pawson win the Marathon in '33. "Les was the one that put me on to him," Johnny says. "He used to send us postcards with training schedules written on them. I'd go into the jewelry store and talk with him. He was more of an advisor than a coach. He'd guide us along until we knew what the running game was all about."

Johnny also enlisted the help of his neighbor, Angus J. MacDonald. Angus was a massage therapist at the McLean Hospital in nearby Belmont. "He was an old bachelor and I was kind of like a son to him. He used to give me all kinds of special treatments. Spine massages and rubdowns, treatments to toughen my feet. McLean is a psychiatric hospital. I wasn't a patient, I was a visitor," Johnny jokes. "Dr. Kenneth Tillotson was the boss. I was allowed to go in any time I wanted."

Done in by blisters in '34, Johnny also decided to do something about his running shoes. "There was no Nike or New Balance back then. In the early days we'd try almost anything—sneakers, bowling shoes. The shoes I finished second in were indoor high-jump shoes—they were black and they were too tight, so I took a razor blade and made slits in the toes on each shoe. In the back of the shoe was a very hard counter and I used to take Neatsfoot oil every night and kind of soften that counter up. The poorest running shoes manufactured today would be far better than anything we had years ago. Then along came an elderly man named Mr. Ritchings, who lived in Lynn. Clarence DeMar and Jock Semple told me about him. He would make a wooden last for your foot only. And around it he'd put this white kid leather, and he'd make a wonderful 5½ ounce shoe—for $7.50."

Samuel T. A. Ritchings called his shoes S.T.A.R. Streamlines. Working in a shack behind his house, he sewed in a piece of elastic that stretched across the top of the shoe. This he called the "goring." Shoestrings were laced through eyelets on the side so they could be tightened without pinching the foot. They were white to reflect the heat. He made them perforated to provide ventilation and he did away with the heel counter that often caused irritation.

"They were his own design, really snug. They were super. One year, eight of the first ten finishers at Boston wore his shoes. Before he died, he sold the business to Osborne K. Winslow—O.K. Winslow—and O.K. made them for a few years."

Tired of internal squabbling, Johnny left the North Medford Club. Except for two stints when he represented the Edison Employees Club, he would run unaffiliated for more than forty years. "I decided to run unattached—with a big 'U' on my chest," Johnny says, winking, "and 'the heck with U' on the back."

Johnny's more businesslike approach to training began to bear fruit. He won several important ten milers and in March successfully defended his title at the North Medford 20 miler, breaking his own course record by over five minutes. Johnny would come to dominate the North Medford race, winning five straight years, eight times overall. A few weeks after North Medford, Johnny finally found regular work, as a florist's assistant in the greenhouses of the G.O. Anderson Florist Shop on Massachusetts Avenue in Arlington. He was also picking up a few dollars by allowing a group of doctors from the Harvard Fatigue Laboratory to include him in a study they were conducting. "They'd put me on the treadmill, check my lungs. They paid me a dollar an hour."

A week or so before the Marathon, Johnny began to feel the tension of being a pre-race favorite. "Because I was an Arlington boy— metropolitan Boston—there was a lot of pressure on me since I'd come in second the year before and won North Medford. To try and get away from it, I went in to Boston the afternoon before the race to see a movie and be alone for a while. I saw Fred Astaire in *Roberta*. It was nice to get away from all the hullabaloo."

The 1935 Boston Marathon was held on Good Friday, a day on which Catholics always ate fish. Johnny had gone to his parish priest, Father James Grimes, and asked for special dispensation so he could have his traditional pre-marathon meal of a thick steak, which his mother always prepared. Father Grimes assured Johnny this was permissible.

After his meal, Johnny made the trip up to Lucky Rock Manor, the formal name for Tebeau's Farm in Hopkinton. Old Man Tebeau would move all the first floor furniture out of his big white farm house onto the lawn and the runners would take the place over, cooking two-inch steaks in the kitchen, eating fried eggs on the staircase. "The B.A.A. used to rent it for $50," Johnny says. "There were runners upstairs, downstairs, all over the place, changing their clothes, pinning numbers on. Plus all the reporters and race officials. Tebeau earned his money. The runners used to leave a real mess behind."

After the required physical examination, wearing #2 pinned to his shirt, Johnny joined the rest of the 190 runners at the start. Dave Komonen, the previous year's winner, was favored to repeat. "But," says Johnny, "I really expected to win the race. I could feel it in my bones. Clarence DeMar used to say you can feel these things coming on and I think it's true. We were lined up at the start and Komonen was beside me, and in his broken English he said, 'You win, you win.' "

In his hand Johnny clutched a handkerchief to wipe his brow. It had been made for him by his Aunt Bessie, an invalid stricken with polio. Pinned inside his trunks was a pouch of white glucose pills given to him by the Harvard scientists he'd been working for as a guinea pig. At noon the gun was fired and Johnny, Komonen and sev-

eral others settled into a pack behind Tony Paskell. At Wellesley
College Johnny, followed closely by Komonen, overtook Paskell.
Near the B.A.A. checkpoint at Wellesley Square, Komonen suddenly fell off the pace and started to walk. The defending champion
would run just a half-mile more before flagging a ride back to
Boston. So certain was Komonen of Johnny's win, he left a congratu-
latory note for Johnny at the Hotel Lenox before leaving town.

But the race wasn't won yet. Frank "Pat" Dengis of Baltimore
mounted a challenge, taking a brief lead before suffering a stitch.
Dengis and Johnny ran in tandem through Wellesley Hills. Johnny
moved ahead on the long downhill stretch into Newton Lower Falls,
a margin he would widen rushing up and down the Newton hills.
Johnny ran alone for the last five miles, maintaining a 300-yard lead.
The crowds, somewhat smaller than usual because of Good Friday
church services, cheered the little local hero along. Johnny's brother
Jimmy was now a crime reporter for the *Boston Traveler* and was riding in a press car (as he would for many years), urging his big brother along.

Approaching Kenmore Square, with a mere mile or so to go,
Johnny began to pale and sicken. There, in the middle of Beacon
Street, he suddenly stopped and doubled over. The crowd went
silent. Johnny had taken too many glucose pills along the route.
Instead of sustaining him, they were about to rob him of victory. Pat
Dengis was closing the gap. Spurred by the pleading crowd, Johnny
started to run again, but stopped, after just a few yards. The crowd
groaned. Without ceremony, Johnny forced a finger down his throat.

"I threw everything up, I was so sick. That was the end of the glucose pills. Once I got rid of them I felt like I could run all the way to
South Boston."

Free of the pills, Johnny sped toward the finish. Rushing down
Exeter Street, he dropped his Aunt Bessie's lucky handkerchief but
continued across the line and into the outstretched arms of his proud
papa. "My father said it was the proudest day of his life. It was my
proudest day too. Graham McNamee was a famous announcer and
he was there broadcasting to the whole country!" Johnny had clocked
the second-fastest time ever run on the course: 2:32:07. His bout
with nausea had cost him the record. The traditional laurel wreath, a
gift each year from the people of Greece, hadn't arrived yet, so a sub-

stitute wreath was plopped on Johnny's head. (The real thing, said in those days to come from a hillside near Athens, arrived two weeks later.)

Johnny was ushered into the jammed, smoke-filled B.A.A. clubhouse for his post-race physical. With his father and four brothers beside him, he answered questions for the newspapers and radio and smiled for pictures. "Last year," he told reporters, "it was 'Rata Auki!' This year it's 'Faugh-a-ballough!'—'Clear the way!' in Gaelic."

After getting showered and dressed, Johnny received his prize: a gold medal adorned with a diamond. Urged to make a speech, he was too emotional to talk. After the ceremony, staff from the *Boston American* wanted to take some exclusive pictures to accompany their story. They drove the new champion and his family down to Warmuth's Restaurant, where a plate of chicken was placed on the table in front of Johnny for a publicity shot. "Wait a minute," Johnny's father said. "This is Good Friday, and my boy is not going to be seen eating meat." Though the picture wasn't going to appear until the next day, William Kelley insisted. The chicken was taken away and Johnny posed with a piece of haddock on his plate.

George H. Lowe, Jr., chairman of the Arlington board of selectmen, summoned a town police car to Warmuth's and Johnny rode home with his father and brother Bill. Once they hit the town line the police siren was turned on, announcing the hero's arrival. The Arlington Fire Department rang the fire bell 39 times in honor of Johnny's win in the 39th B.A.A. race. Johnny's mother and sisters met him at the door. The rest of the night the phone kept ringing and well wishers kept dropping by. Neighbor children were peering in the windows. A telegram came from Governor James M. Curley.

A few weeks later a testimonial was held at the high school auditorium. Clarence DeMar and Jimmy Henigan came; so did Governor Curley. A song was sung to the tune of "Easter Parade," a fitting selection, since the morning after his triumph Johnny Kelley was back at Anderson's Florist Shop, potting Easter lilies.

That morning, Johnny didn't really get much work done, though he arrived by 7:30, a half-hour earlier than usual. Reporters, admirers, and autograph seekers all converged on Anderson's, which was loaded with Easter lilies. The *Traveler* posed Johnny for a picture with his co-workers and some Palmer Street neighbors who'd stopped by. Even Elmer Anderson, who ran the business with his brother, smiled and dallied with the press.

One of the reporters who showed up at Anderson's that morning was 26-year-old Paul "Jerry" Nason of the *Boston Globe*. Jerry Nason would become the Boston Marathon's foremost historian. He covered the race for the *Globe* for fifty years, maintaining a bulging scrapbook, meticulous lists of checkpoint records and a cache of photographs. "He wrote up a lot of wonderful articles about me," Johnny recalls, "gave me a lot of ink over the years. I owe him a lot of thank yous."

1935 was the year sports editor Victor O. Jones chose Jerry to become the *Globe*'s new track and Marathon writer. Jerry first reported the race in 1932, when his assignment was to stake out a phone booth at Kenmore Square and call into the paper the probable winner, so they could start setting the headlines. But his love for the Marathon went all the way back to boyhood. He saw his first Boston as a schoolboy in 1920, standing by the road watching the runners pass over the hills of Newton, his hometown. Or at least that's the first one he remembered seeing. Born April 14, 1909, at the old Newton-Framingham Hospital overlooking the course, five-day-old Jerry, the story goes, was held up to the window as the runners were passing through town by a nurse whose boyfriend was running in the race.

At a time when most writers looked upon the Marathon as little more than a sideshow, Jerry Nason took the race seriously and wrote about it in a tone that was light but dignified. Gradually, other writers followed Jerry's lead. "Of all the sports he wrote about," Johnny says, "baseball, football—whatever—Jerry loved the Marathon the best." Indeed, during his long tenure Jerry Nason covered far more than marathons. He reported on six World Series, five Olympic Games, all of Rocky Marciano's title fights, several Super Bowls, and scores of college football games. But his favorite athletes were always the marathoners, those bricklayers, plumbers, milkmen, and carpenters who, instead of resting after their day's labor, chose to train and compete. Even after he formally retired from the *Globe* in 1974, Jerry continued to cover the Marathon for another nine years. "Everything he wrote was authentic. No one loved the running game more than Jerry Nason."

Kelley at Work 7:30 Morning after Triumph
Boston Globe, April 21, 1935
by Jerry Nason

A stone's toss from the Arlington High School stands the florist establishment of the Anderson brothers, its flowered front facing Massachusetts Avenue and its huge green houses reaching in a long chain to the rear.

Yesterday morning at 7:30 a little man in a suede sport jacket and a gray sweat shirt trudged to the rear entrance, lunch bag under one arm, to commence his day's work.

It was Johnny Kelley, the Arlington Irishman with the twinkling eye and the chipmunk's saucy grin, who, 19 hours before, had led a crack field of distance runners over 26 miles in the annual Boston A.A. Marathon.

"I feel great, simply great," he chortled. "I still can't believe it all. I'm not letting it fool me, though," he hastened to add. "This is fleeting fame. No one knows it better than I do. I will live the same, feel the same and think the same. But boy, it sure is a swell feeling to be the Marathon winner."

Little Chance To Work

How like Johnny Kelley to turn up for work the next morning after his popular triumph ready for his various duties in, around and outside the vast greenhouses—and a half-hour early for work.

"He didn't have to do it," informed Elmer Anderson, one of the brother proprietors. "Johnny," he offered, as he turned to the little fellow who made his establishment a mecca for hero-worshipping school children, autograph-seeking persons and curious customers yesterday, "anytime you want to take time off, you take it and come back later.

"I couldn't see any of the race myself yesterday," he

remarked sadly, "but all of us here were confident
Johnny would win it. He was determined all last week
that he'd win. He's a great boy, too."

Although he officially reported for work, Kelley did-
n't get much of a chance to labor yesterday. Phone
calls, pencil wielders of the press, photographers, bear-
ers of congratulations formed an unsurmountable barrier to business.

On the sidewalk knots of eager schoolboys formed,
anxious to snatch a glimpse of the Marathon champion
as his black thatch bobbed among the stately lilies. Two
little girls slipped timidly through the door. "May we
have your autograph, Mr. Kelley?" a bashful, shy
request from one with a red ribbon.

Hid From Talk at Movie

The Kelley boy was in perfect condition. "Without
meaning to boast, Jerry," was his observation, "I felt 30
or 40 percent better in the North Medford 20 miler in
March than I did even yesterday. I had more zip, more
pep that day than at any time during the B.A.A. race.

"One thing that helped me win yesterday was that
the real experts weren't picking me. I know that would
have been a mental handicap, knowing that the men
who knew running were picking me. Komonen was the
fellow to beat. I was awfully nervous a few days before
the race, as you will remember. All my friends meant
well, but all I heard for days was Marathon, Marathon,
Marathon.

"The day before the race I went to a movie in Boston
all by myself. It was a good show and for three hours I
sat there forgetting all about the Marathon and hearing
nothing about it. Let me tell you it was a relief and a
rest as well."

Kelley is contented with his position, which he has
held for nearly three weeks.

"No, I never had been particularly interested in
flowers before I came here, but say, aren't they pretty,

though? It sort of gets you somehow. And it's healthy work, interesting and the day just seems to fly by."

A very religious lad, Kelley is also an exceptionally clean living and clean thinking person. It is not assumed. It is natural with his entire family.

To Take Mother West

Speaking of families, Johnny claims his is the best in the whole wide world. "My mother was so happy I think she cried. And my father was tickled pink. I hope he doesn't spoil me. Gee, they are great rooters, my brothers and sisters.

"I think I have a chance to run in San Diego this summer with all expenses paid and I'm going to take my mother along with me. She was born in Juanita, Nebraska and lived there as a little girl before coming to Lunenburg. She has never been back to Juanita since and this will be a great chance, if it turns out they want me to run there.

"Al Monteverde wrote me from the Coast recently and said that if I made a good showing in the B.A.A. race they wanted me to run there. Haven't heard from him since, though."

Well, you simply are seeing the real Johnny Kelley when you learn how his first thoughts are for his mother when offered an invitation such as this.

So I left him a still slightly bewildered young man among the posies, but one who will let the brief glory slide off his shoulders like rain from a barn roof.

Johnny Kelley will wear well.

Chapter 4
HEARTBREAK HILL GETS ITS NAME

For a large family during the Depression, all the attention Johnny gained through his running success made a difficult time a bit more bearable. Along with his father and brothers and sisters, a crowd of Kelley cousins, uncles, and aunts always turned out for Johnny's big races. All four of his younger brothers are gone now, but Johnny's sisters still savor many happy moments.

"In our dining room we had a small alcove, a breakfast nook," remembers Johnny's sister Mary. "My father made it into a display area for all of Johnny's trophies and medals. He even had Johnny's laurel wreath preserved in wax and framed. Every April the press would start to show up at the house to talk to Johnny. My mother would say, 'Don't you think it's time to shine your brother's trophies?' Ruthie and I were the youngest, so we'd polish them up. Johnny always gave us a dime for doing it."

"My father was very proud of Johnny," recalls sister Marion. "He went to nearly every race and always greeted Johnny at the finish line with open arms and a warm blanket."

William Kelley became son Johnny's biggest fan. "I didn't find out about it 'til years later," Johnny says, "but my brother Bill told me that, in '35, my father made everybody kneel down and say a prayer for me at 12 o'clock noon, which is the time the Marathon starts."

"Our mother was the nervous type," says sister Ruth. "She'd

worry about Johnny's physical condition so she rarely went to races. But she'd listen to the Marathon on the radio. We'd call her from the Hotel Lenox near the finish line and let her know Johnny was okay. She wrote a poem about Johnny. I've kept it all these years."

Marathon Time
It may be springtime in the Rockies
But it's Marathon time out here.
The house is all a-flutter,
It's in the atmosphere,
And Johnny's out practicing
Along the Mystic River track
And thinking how on Patriots' Day
He'll run and lead the pack.
The house is very noisy,
The phone rings all the day
And the doorbell keeps us hustling,
So many visitors our way.
It's Johnny here and it's Johnny on the air
And he goes around like mad,
It's a most exciting time,
When it's over he'll be glad!
It keeps me busy preparing his meals
And cooking them to order everyday
The oatmeal, steaks and crackers,
Grapefruit and bananas.
If he wins, that will be my pay!!
Yes, it may be springtime in the Rockies
But it's Marathon time out here
If you don't believe it
Just take a peak inside.
You'll see photographers and reporters
From the newspapers in town.
They come to see my Johnny
And all his praise they sound.
Oh it's a busy place out here
And there's much excitement, too!
But we're all having lots of fun
And hope he wins, don't you?

"Johnny would bring runners home all the time and my mother would always feel sorry for them and let them stay for dinner," remembers Ruth. "We used to ask Johnny if he was going to open a home for all the destitute runners. Of course today the top runners are getting all kinds of money."

"Johnny was always a good-living boy," says sister Margaret. "He never got into any real trouble. He would go around the house singing like Bing Crosby, and he'd sound like him too. We used to tell him he would make a good stand-in for Crosby and he'd just laugh. Johnny was a very happy fellow."

"Sometimes before a race, though, Johnny would get very edgy," says Mary. "He'd try to get to sleep early but my other brothers would fill the bed with barbells, spiked running shoes and a flatiron. Johnny would start yelling, pretending he was mad. But we were all proud of our big brother. Johnny gave me a Waltham watch he won at a race one time, and I still have it."

On Thanksgiving Day, 1935, the Yonkers Marathon was revived after an eighteen-year absence from what was then a meager list of marathons in the United States. "Now there's hundreds of marathons each year, but there were only four or five regular ones back then," Johnny says, "Boston, Yonkers, Washington, D.C., and Port Chester." Yonkers was a beautiful course, but loaded with roller-coaster hills. It started with a one-mile lap around the Empire City Race Track, normally reserved for horses, and concluded with four more miles around the raceway. "It was like running on beach sand. Les Pawson had a leg cramp up on him and that helped me win. I only ran Yonkers because they told me it was an Olympic trial. It wasn't."

In March of 1936 Johnny again captured the North Medford 20 miler. The stage seemed set for a repeat win at Boston, which would be the first of two Olympic trials. Since his popular Boston victory, the Berlin Games had become Johnny's goal. Most Boston newspapers—there were seven or eight at the time—favored him to repeat, or listed him as a co-favorite with Pat Dengis, who had hounded Johnny to the finish the previous year. Dengis had also won the 1935 national championship. The *Globe's* Jerry Nason, however, picked neither, instead opting for a long shot named Ellison Meyers "Tarzan" Brown. A Narragansett Indian from Rhode Island, Brown had won a pair of national championships at 20 and 25 kilometers, but had yet to distinguish himself in the marathon. Just 22 years old, Brown had run Boston the previous year wearing a jersey made by his sisters, cut from the cloth of a dress that belonged to his mother, who had died two weeks earlier. The sneakers he had worn fell apart, and he ran the last five miles barefoot, placing thirteenth.

Nicknamed "Tarzan" by his boyhood friends because of his love for climbing trees and hollering like vine-swinger Johnny Weissmuller, Ellison Brown was perhaps the greatest physical specimen to compete in the Boston Marathon. Blessed with outstanding speed and strength, he lived in rural poverty his entire life, and trained erratically, often substituting wood-chopping for distance work. These days he is remembered more for his unpredictable antics than his unbridled running prowess. Jerry Nason came upon him in Hopkinton once, wolfing down several hot dogs just minutes before the race. "I didn't have any breakfast," Brown explained, washing the dogs down with soda pop. Brown was also known to hold back in a race if the second or third place prize was more salable. "You can't eat trophies," he said.

When the gun reported, Tarzan Brown flew away from the start as if he were running a dash. His pace was so outrageous that the press cars followed the wrong runners for five miles, mistaking them for the leaders. Shattering checkpoint records at every turn, the young Indian had a 900-yard lead heading into the hills of Newton but he was beginning to pay for his foolish gallop. Not wanting to take the chance that Brown might fade and come back to him, Johnny gave chase. Erasing a half-mile lead with one of the most furious runs through the hills in history, Johnny finally pulled even with Brown near the top of the last hill near Boston College. As he passed, Johnny gave the flagging Tarzan a friendly pat on the shoulder as if to say, "Nice try, kid. I'll take it from here."

But Johnny's lead was short-lived. Tarzan Brown, incited by Johnny's well-meaning tap, suddenly summoned enough strength to speed past Johnny, who was now feeling the effects of his mad pursuit through the hills. They came down off the hill with Brown back in the lead. Between Lake Street and Cleveland Circle Johnny made one last desperate surge past Brown, who remained expressionless through it all, as if running in a trance. But now Johnny was utterly spent. Brown eventually passed him a second and final time.

Both runners began weaving like punched-out prize fighters.

On Beacon Street, William "Biddie" McMahon of Worcester overtook Johnny. A mile and a half from the finish, Brown began walking, so disoriented that he was almost struck by a car. McMahon was within 75 yards of Tarzan, but he too began to walk, depleted by his efforts to catch the two leaders. Two hundred yards back, Johnny was also walking, unable to muster a final challenge.

Tarzan, doused with water by one of his handlers, began to run again. He stopped once more at Kenmore Square, but somehow revived himself and then hobbled home in 2:33:40. McMahon, with a weak trot, held on to second place. Johnny gutted out the last mile, but was overhauled by Mel Porter and Leo Giard. He crossed the line in 2:38:49 and was carried away to the dressing room. "All I had to do was run a minute slower than I was going," Johnny says, looking back, "and I would've gone right by Tarzan at the end. But he was so far ahead—I used very, very poor judgment and I'm man enough to admit that."

When asked about this race late in his life, the disappointment was still evident in Johnny's blue-green eyes, though it occurred more than 56 years ago. It was that same crestfallen gaze that Jerry Nason, riding in the *Globe*'s press car, saw in Johnny's eyes on the final Newton hill, prompting Nason to name that hill "Heartbreak." The name has become part of the Boston Marathon's mystique, but most people assume this last incline is called Heartbreak because it lies just past the twenty-mile mark, where most runners begin to weaken. It is named instead for one fearless little man, Johnny Kelley, whose heart was indeed broken there—but not his indomitable spirit.

John Kelley as a member of the 1924 Medford High School track team. (John Kelley Collection)

Inset: Johnny spent four splendid summers working as a caddy in the White Mountains of New Hampshire. (John Kelley Collection)

The lead pack in the 1932 Boston Marathon is shown leaving the Framingham check-point. Pictured are
(l-r) Les Pawson, Jim Henigan, Bill Steiner, Alex Burnside, and Johnny Kelley. Kelley would drop out at Wellesley due to blisters. (John Kelley Collection)

Les Pawson battled the fiercest headwinds in Boston Marathon history to win the 1933 race in record time. It was the first of his three Boston triumphs. (Les Pawson Collection)

Joie Ray, the ``Kankakee Kid,'' was one of Johnny Kelley's early idols.

In the 1930s, the Boston Globe covered the Boston Marathon from this 1934 Studebaker President. Pictured are (l-r) Norbert Quinn, Jerry Nason, Victor Hones, Charles McCormick, and Zachary Shore. (Jerry Nason Collection)

Dave Komonen leads Kelley in the stretch drive of the 1934 Boston Marathon. This race would be the first of Kelley's seven second place finishes. (John Kelley Collection)

Kelley can't help but grin as he passes the women of Wellesley College near the halfway mark of the 1935 Boston Marathon. He was pursued by Bernat Malm (#175) and 1934 winner Dave Komonen (#1). (*Boston Globe*)

Here, Kelley has just crossed the finish line of the 1935 Marathon in front of the Lenox Hotel on Exeter Street. Note the shamrock pinned to his singlet. (*Boston Globe*)

Famed announcer Graham McNamee couldn't be closer to the action as he informs the nation of Kelley's Boston victory. (*Boston Globe*)

Kelley is crowned with the traditional victor's laurels. (*Boston Globe*)

Inset: Eleven Boston Marathon victories are represented by the runners in this picture.
From left to right they are
Les Pawson with three victories, Clarence DeMar with seven victories, and Jimmy
Henigan with one victory. All three were major influences on Kelley's running career.
(Les Pawson Collection)

The day after his Marathon victory, John Kelley was headline news. (John Kelley Collection)

The Kelley clan is shown gathered at the family's Arlington home on the night of Johnny's first Boston Marathon victory in 1935. Pictured are
(top, l-r) Mattie, Eddie, Marion, Margaret, Jim, Bill, Ruth, (bottom, l-r) William, Johnny, Bertha, Mary, and Katherine. (John Kelley Collection)

In 1935, Kelley won the Boston Marathon on his fifth attempt at the historic race. Here he is shown receiving the victor's laurels from Boston politician and restaurateur George Demeter. (John Kelley Collection)

Paul ``Jerry'' Nason in 1935. Nason reported on the Marathon for the *Boston Globe* for 50 years, and gave Heartbreak Hill its name. (The Sports Museum Collection)

Chapter 5
"MARATHON LAUFER"

$\mathscr{P}$rior to the '36 B.A.A., the strongest candidates for the U.S. Olympic marathon team were Johnny Kelley, Leslie Pawson, Pat Dengis, and Mel Porter. But now nothing could be assumed. Pawson and Dengis had both dropped out of Boston. Tarzan Brown's victory had suddenly assured him a trip to Berlin. Porter's third place finish had strengthened his standing and now there was Biddie McMahon to reckon with. Johnny's fade to fifth further clouded the selection process. A second trial was scheduled for the following month in Washington, D.C. Johnny was reluctant to compete, embarrassed by his loss at Boston but convinced that his record over the last two years should speak for itself. "I was a stubborn guy," Johnny admits. "I thought I deserved to be on the team. But they said I had to run the trial no matter what." Halfheartedly, Johnny entered.

The second trial started at Mount Vernon, followed the Potomac River, and finished at Capitol Hill. Biddie McMahon, who finished second at Boston, won the trial, clinching an Olympic berth. Johnny finished second, thinking that he too had finally won a spot. But Mel Porter was third in both trials, causing the selection committee to waver. The average times for the two trials, 2:39:38 to 2:40:18, favored Johnny slightly. Also, Johnny had won two of his four marathons, beating Porter two of the three times they went head-to-head at that distance. Still, the selection committee stalled. Johnny was dumbfounded. "Overall, I had beaten Porter eleven of the twelve races we'd run. My record was even better than Brown's and McMahon's, never mind Porter's!"

Sportswriters across the country debated the issue. Most supported Johnny. But the selection committee delayed their decision until late June. Johnny was on the job at Anderson's Florist Shop when the call finally came from Bill Bingham of Harvard, chairman of the U.S. Olympic Track Committee. The votes were tallied and Johnny Kelley would be the third man on the marathon team. Mel Porter would be the alternate. Johnny's tactical errors at Boston had almost made him miss the boat to Berlin, but now he could pack his bags.

The U.S. Olympic team left New York City on the *Manhattan,* bound for Hamburg, Germany. The voyage would take about seven days. "It was one big happy family," Johnny remembers. "Today the Olympic teams fly—zoom, and they're there. They don't get to know one another. We had a great time going over on the boat. Glenn Cunningham, the famous mile runner, was on the boat with us. Tarzan had brought an Indian headdress with him, so one day Cunningham went over and said, 'Hey Tarz, can I pose with you?' He put his arm around Tarzan and posed for pictures. Tarzan was the proudest guy on the boat. I met Ralph Metcalfe, the sprinter, and Jesse Owens, the greatest track and field man who ever lived."

James "Jesse" Owens, a Black American, won four gold medals in Berlin, mocking Adolf Hitler's supposed showcase of Aryan supremacy. "Jesse ran all his races without starting blocks," says Johnny. "He had to dig a hole with a trowel. There's no telling what he might have accomplished if he'd had better training, better equipment."

Johnny first met Jesse Owens crossing on the *Manhattan.* Johnny was sitting in the cabin he shared with Tarzan Brown and Biddie McMahon, when Owens came in and saw Johnny's white, custom-made S.T.A.R. Streamlines. "Jesse wanted to put them on and go jogging on deck. Most of us jogged on deck, but it was dangerous. I always worried the ship might roll and I'd turn an ankle. But I did it just the same. Anyway, I told Jesse his foot was much larger than mine but he kept insisting. Finally I said, 'Okay, try 'em on.' Rrrrip! He tore it right down the heel. I found a mate on the ship, a Swede, who stitched it back up. Did a beautiful job. Cost me fifty cents. Jesse was very apologetic. Later he came over to me in the dining hall to see how I made out. I had brought two other pair with me anyway."

Upon reaching Hamburg, the team was transported by double-decker buses to the Olympic village in Doberitz, 10 miles from Berlin. It was at the Olympic village in Doberitz that Johnny met the great Finnish distance runner, Paavo Nurmi.

"I was 28, Nurmi was 38, over his peak. He was the Finnish coach. He was kinda cold to me when I first went up to him, then he said, 'What's your name?'

"'Kelley.'

"'Oh!'

"He grabbed ahold of me—he was so excited. I couldn't believe it! To me he was God, ya know. Geez, we had quite a talk. The fact that he knew who I was—geez.

"Each day I'd go out for a run and one of Hitler's youth corps would escort me on his bicycle and stop traffic for me. One day I went to the stadium to watch some of the other events, and a truck pulled up with a group of German soldiers in it. They were all huge men, all over six feet tall, wearing their steel helmets. One of them spoke pretty good English. I wore 'U.S.A.' on my chest so he asked me for some American cigarettes. Then one of them took my straw hat off and put his steel helmet on my head. It slid down almost to my chin and they got a laugh out of that. They didn't believe I was an athlete. I only weighed 122 pounds. He asked me if I was on the checkers or tiddlywinks team.

"They kept taunting me and I started to get upset. I told the one who spoke English I was a marathon runner. He told them, 'Marathon laufer. 42,000 meters.' They looked at me different after that. It was one of the proudest moments of my life. They respected me because I was a marathon man. They asked me if I knew Paul deBruyn, a German who won Boston in 1932. I said, 'Sure, I know Paul.' Finally they all shook my hand and wished me luck. I found out later they were some of Hitler's bodyguards.

"Hitler was there every day, watching. He looked like Charlie Chaplin sitting up there, him and the fat guy, Goering. Hitler waved at me, but I didn't wave back. According to all the journalists, Hitler snubbed Jesse Owens. But Jesse told me himself that Hitler did wave to him and Jesse waved back."

While Johnny did all of his training around Doberitz, Tarzan Brown did some of his in the German beer gardens and got into a scuffle with some of Hitler's Blackshirts. "I remember one morning I was going to breakfast and Tarzan was just coming into the village. I said, 'Where you been?' and he just kind of grunted and dove in the swimming pool."

Tarzan Brown ran the Olympic marathon with a hernia. "Tarz was just ahead of me getting his physical before the race, and the doctor told him, 'You'd better get this taken care of, son.' Tarz just said, 'Naw, doesn't bother me.' "

On August 9th, at 3 P.M., Johnny joined the 56 other competitors on the red clay track, wearing his woolen U.S.A. jersey. "Those shirts were like sandpaper," Johnny recalls. "On a hot day they chafed you all over. Tarzan Brown wouldn't wear his. Even the 5,000- and 10,000-meter men complained."

Johnny even had his own cheering section at Berlin. His father made the trip, along with his brother Jimmy who was on his honeymoon. An added surprise was the arrival of Johnny's brother Bill, whose co-workers at the State of Massachusetts Tax Office had taken up a collection so he could go. After one lap around the track the runners left the Reich Sports Field and Stadium. The course was hilly, mostly wooded, thirteen miles out, thirteen back. German soldiers lined much of the route. Johnny was never a serious contender for the lead, "I finished eighteenth, which is no great shakes on my part, but I gave it everything I had. I told my father and brothers I'd finish if I had to walk in."

Johnny was the only American to finish. Along the way he came upon Tarzan Brown, who was standing by the road rubbing his leg. " 'Too tough for me today,' he said as I went by." Actually Brown had been disqualified when a man had tried to help him massage a painful cramp. Since his win at Boston in April, Tarzan had done little training. Still, he had been with the leaders for thirteen miles. But his inexperience and lack of conditioning betrayed him. The winner was Sohn Kee-chung, a Korean. (His country occupied by imperialist Japan, he was forced to compete under his Japanese name.)

When Johnny returned to the stadium, he was spent. "We entered through a dark tunnel and when we came out it was so bright I was blinded. I thought I might crash into one of the huge concrete pillars that supported the grandstands." His sandpaper-like shirt had rubbed his chest raw and his nipples were bleeding. "I collapsed on the grass. Two German soldiers grabbed me by my arms and yanked me off the field. They almost pulled my arms off. They didn't mean any harm. The rule was you had to leave the field once your event was over."

The marathon was, as always, the final event of the Olympiad. When their ship docked in New York, the athletes were welcomed by the great heavyweight boxer, Jack Dempsey, who served as the official greeter. Johnny shook his hand. A ticker-tape parade was held on Broadway but Johnny didn't participate. "I was welcome to be in it, but I hadn't done well, so I wanted to go home."

Except for a fourth-place finish in a 1949 event in Oslo, Norway—at the age of 42—Johnny never fared well in international competition. Running two marathon trials in two months just before the Games didn't help in Berlin. "In '48 we had to run *three* trials! I never kibitzed with any of the European runners about their training. Even the more experienced runners at home never talked much about what they did. They told me what *I* should do," Johnny says, "but never said what *they* did."

With the '36 Olympics now a treasured memory, Johnny set his sights on redeeming his dismal defeat at Boston. He had left the Anderson brothers' employ. "They liked me at Anderson's, but I was only making $3.00 a day. I quit and went back to odd jobs. I worked in a department store for a while, then I went back to Leonard Collins' gas station part-time."

Gearing up for Boston at the North Medford 20 miler, Johnny won for the fourth straight year, taking more than two minutes off his own course record. Finishing an impressive but distant second was a lean, long-legged Canadian named Walter Young. Tall for a marathoner at nearly six feet, Young had stayed with Johnny for 14 miles before stomach problems slowed him down. Like Johnny, he was sporadically employed. His wife and child, back in the city of Verdun, were living on relief. He had come to Boston thinking that if he could win the Marathon he might also win enough notoriety to interest someone in giving him a job. He had come in 26th the year before, but his second place finish at North Medford further fueled his dream.

Young came to Boston a month before the race to train on the course with his coach, Pete Gavuzzi, a veteran of C.C. Pyle's 3,000-mile Bunion Derbies from Los Angeles to New York. Gavuzzi prescribed frequent two- and three-hour runs for his protégés. Young, who was also a snowshoe champion, logged 100-mile weeks in practice, far more than most marathoners of the day. A week before the Marathon, Young and Gavuzzi's money ran out. The Castor Athletic Club of Montreal had not come through with promised support. Young took the Waltham watch he'd won at North Medford and pawned it for $7.00. He returned to Verdun and called on Herve Ferland, the mayor. Young convinced Ferland to give him the money to return to Boston. He also got the mayor to make him a promise. "He did tell me that if I made good in winning the Boston Marathon," remembered Young at age 79, "that I would get a position on the Verdun Police Department." Walter Young arrived back in Boston the night before the race.

Johnny found himself the heavy favorite despite the fact that six former winners would join him at Lucky Rock Manor, so-called because of a great rock ledge that was situated on the property. Defending champion Tarzan Brown was in the field of 169, but his status was uncertain. He had only recently resumed training after surgery. (Embarrassed by his poor showing at Berlin, Brown had stunned everyone when he ran and won two full-distance marathons on successive days. First the angry Indian set the course record in Port Chester, New York; then he took the train to Manchester, New Hampshire, where he again set a new mark. After this amazing "double," Brown was out training on a back road one day and collapsed. If a passerby hadn't found him, Tarzan might have died. The hernia the doctor had warned him about in Berlin was double strangulated.)

Almost from the gun, Johnny could feel Young hanging on his shoulder as the lead pack gradually began to thin. "Johnny was the best in the game perhaps at that time," says the soft-spoken Young. "On one occasion he reached to the side, got a cup of water and handed it over to me—very sportsmanlike in that sort of instance." The two made an awkward pair. Young's stride was long and ungainly, Johnny's efficient and graceful. Young wore a red maple leaf across his chest. Johnny's jersey was white with a small green shamrock over his heart. Over a twelve-mile stretch these two underemployed front runners would exchange the lead sixteen times, defying each other as well as the 75-degree heat. Leslie Pawson managed to trail close behind as far as Auburndale, but lost contact as they approached the hills.

Going up the first Newton hill, Johnny put 60 yards between himself and Young. "Right there I thought I had the race won," Johnny told Jerry Nason after the race. "I felt strong. I figured it was just a question of running through to the finish." But coming down the first slope, Johnny began to suffer stomach troubles. Four times he had to stop and purge his ailing stomach. Young seized the lead. At North Medford a month earlier it had been Young's stomach that had rebelled.

Johnny gathered himself and gamely sped after his lanky opponent, attacking the hills. They were fast approaching the spot where Johnny had caught the wilting Tarzan Brown the year before. Again Johnny chose to challenge on the final hill. This time there was no friendly pat on the shoulder, nothing to arouse the weary Canadian. Johnny passed Young and crested Heartbreak Hill. When he hit Lake Street he appeared home free. He opened a 100-yard lead that was enhanced by a parade of press cars and motorcycles that blocked Johnny from Young's view.

The crowd, estimated at 500,000, rooted the local boy on. But as he approached 23 miles, Johnny's nervous stomach and aggressive charge over the hills took their toll. At Coolidge Corner Young reclaimed the lead. His superior strength carried him the last three miles to the finish and to the steady employment he'd been promised. The race lost, Johnny bravely plodded home on sheer willpower. "How I got in from Coolidge Corner I don't know," Johnny told reporters after the race. "I think I chased him too fast over the hills, after I lost the lead. I should have known better. The same thing cost me the race last year." Each man had suffered from the struggle, Johnny losing eight pounds from his already slight frame, Young dropping ten. Johnny graciously posed for pictures with Young, masking his regret. "Young ran a strong, willing race. He has my sincerest congratulations," he said.

Despite the numbing loss at Boston, 1937 was a good year for

Johnny. In May he won the National A.A.U. 15-kilometer race by nearly a quarter of a mile. In August he added the National 25-kilometer championship. He also displayed his speed, taking the New England three-mile outdoor title. But unlike Walter Young, whose victory had brought him steady employment that would last for the next 41 years, Johnny was still floundering, working part-time at Leonard Collins' gas station. He spoke openly to the press about his plight, but no offers resulted. Leonard Collins, a former Arlington selectman, suggested to Johnny that he approach Tom Carens, assistant to the president of the New England Power Association. Carens, who gassed up at Collins' pumps, had attended the testimonial for Johnny after he won Boston in '35.

Johnny went down to see Carens and filled out an application. "One day I came home from the movies and my mother said, 'They want to see you.' I went down there and I got hired. I worked at the power station in South Boston. My first job was as a security guard. Later, after I returned from the service, I became a mechanical maintenance man. Hard physical labor. In the boiler room, out on the dock, up on the roof, everywhere. But it was forty hours a week and I was very fortunate. It wasn't a healthy place to work. I turned down a lot of overtime. In those days we didn't know how bad asbestos is. I did a lot of work with asbestos. Many a time I had to wear a mask. I didn't do asbestos work all the time, but I did a lot of it. I'm fortunate I didn't become infected. I read the Edison newsletter and one after the other, all the men I worked with are gone. My wife says it's because I'd go out and run at night in the fresh air. I just say I was lucky, that's all. Very lucky.

"I don't know how Les Pawson and myself and all the other runners were able to maintain good condition and run good races holding down a physical 8-hour-a-day job and training at night in the cold and dark and rain," Johnny says, shaking his head. "I'd go to work in the morning and see people running along the Charles River and wish I could be out there. I tried it a few times, but it made me too tired on the job. I'd come home from work exhausted all the time— I'd never feel like running. But I'd force myself out there and by the end of the run I'd feel refreshed. Maybe the job toughened me up. There was a lot of walking and bending and climbing and stooping, ya know."

1937 was also the year the incomparable Clarence H. DeMar, seven-time winner of the Boston Marathon, published his autobiography. "Gosh-hemlocks! I had great admiration for Clarence because of his seven Boston wins. He wasn't very fast. He won all his races on determination," Johnny says. "He used to work all night at the *Herald* as a printer and then run the Marathon the next day. He was from the old—very old—school. He was a very honest, outspoken man. Sometimes he could be abrupt, very sharp. You couldn't get too friendly with him. He was very sarcastic, but he gave me some good advice—I bought his book. DeMar had an awkward style, not very pretty, but he'd get there. His feet would slap the pavement. He made an awful racket. You could really hear him coming. He used to say, 'Run like hell and get the agony over with.' "

DeMar had dominated the Marathon in the '20s. He was a compositor for many years and later taught typography at the Keene Normal School in New Hampshire. A strict Baptist who believed in a balanced lifestyle, he also taught Sunday school and led a Boy Scout troop. Often belligerent, he would not endure foolish questions from reporters or hesitate to shove a bicycle rider or spectator who got too close. He actually won the race for the first time in 1911. A doctor giving him his pre-race physical told him he had a heart murmur and warned him against competing. He ran the race anyway and set a course record. But after running in the 1912 Olympics in Stockholm, where a Portuguese marathoner collapsed and died a day later, DeMar decided to heed the physician's advice and stop running marathons. He continued running shorter races and resumed his education.

From the age of 23 to 32, his prime competitive years, DeMar returned to the Marathon only once, finishing third. When the doctor who had warned him to quit died of a heart attack himself, DeMar wryly remarked, "He must have been listening to his own heart back then." DeMar started to run the Marathon regularly in 1922, and won it six times over the next nine races. It is mind-boggling to ponder how many laurel wreaths he might have collected had he not skipped his optimum years.

"The Marathon is a different race than it was in DeMar's day," Johnny says. "It's a speed race now and the competition is too fierce for anyone to win it seven times. Our records are actually reversed you know. DeMar was first seven times and second twice, I won it twice and was seven times second."

DeMar competed in three Olympic Games, winning a bronze medal in Paris in '24. His last Boston win was in 1930, just before his 42nd birthday. All told, he ran 33 Boston Marathons, not stopping until the age of 66, four years before his death from intestinal cancer. DeMar was in some ways the first grand old man of the Marathon. "The crowds used to wait for Clarence to pass by," Johnny says. "Now they wait for me."

Will Cloney, 80, a Boston sports reporter for 26 years and race director of the B.A.A. Marathon for 35 years, says, "They waited for DeMar, but not the way they wait for Johnny. DeMar 'til the day he died was a loner. He had a strange disposition. I worked at the *Herald* with him and I'd go down to see him to get a story and he'd barely give me the time of day. Johnny is really an endearing figure. DeMar was remote. I don't think anybody'd wait around four or five hours for DeMar the way they do for Johnny."

In 1938 Johnny won the North Medford 20 miler for the fifth consecutive year. He had become almost unbeatable at distances of ten to twenty miles. "My favorite distance was about 15 miles. My running in the marathon—after about 18-20 miles I needed a kiss and a prayer to keep going, I guess. I didn't have the strength these other fellas had. *Determination* I had."

At North Medford, Johnny's competition was supplied by a surprise entry, Gerard Armand Cote, a fun-loving French Canadian who was staying with relatives in Taunton, preparing for the Marathon. Cote came from St. Hyacinthe, a farming town east of Montreal. His mischievous smile was accented by two shining, gold-capped teeth. Like his countryman Walter Young, Cote was trained by Pete Gavuzzi and favored long training runs of up to 35 miles. He, too, logged 100-mile weeks. Also like Young, he was a snowshoe champion.

"Gerry could go all day," Johnny says. Cote, just 24, was the same height as Johnny but eleven pounds heavier. "He was a powerfully built man. He was so strong—he could run 40 or 50 miles if he had to. I know he could. He wasn't very fast, though. Gerry would admit that. I could give him a minute, minute and a half in a ten-mile race and catch him. When he ran he swayed his arms so wide if you didn't watch out you could get an elbow in the belly. He didn't mean to be rough, but you had to keep away from him. When he first started coming around he didn't speak English. But by going to races and talking with the runners he taught himself the language."

On an unusually warm day in March, thousands of spectators came out to see the race. Cote shadowed Johnny the entire way, forcing a sprint at the finish. With a final burst, Johnny won by sixteen seconds. But Gerard Cote was on the rise. In the years to come the lighthearted, cigar-smoking monsieur would win the Boston Marathon four times, a performance second only to DeMar's, equaled only by Bill Rodgers' more than thirty years later. Cote, just before his 79th birthday, remembered, " 'Kellee' was a good friend of mine. A very good friend. We ran together, shoulder to shoulder, never an argument. He'd pass me cups of water. Pawson, same thing. Pat Dengis, Tarzan Brown, same thing—they were all like a gang of brothers to me. And when we were running a race, before the starting gun, we'd always say, 'Best man win.' "

On Patriots' Day, 1938, the thermometer rose to 75 degrees. An estimated million people lined the route and Pat Dengis later swore that most of them must have been Johnny Kelley's relatives, the way they kept urging Johnny along. Walter Young, representing Canada at the Empire Games in Australia, was not there to defend his title. Johnny was now sporting the emblem of the Edison Employees Club, an arrangement that would last about ten years before souring. "The Employees Club talked me into running for them. Well, I thought that was a pretty good thing to do, but all it did was lead to trouble. They used to allocate $25.00 a year for me to buy running shoes or whatever. Then someone said this and someone said that, and I said the heck with it—I'll run unattached; be my own boss."

Johnny took the lead from Duncan McCallum of Toronto after 8 miles, tailed by Leslie Pawson, his good friend. Except for his distant third place finish a year earlier, Pawson had not fared well at Boston since his record-setting run in '33. The two pals ran side-by-side for several miles, sharing cups of water. Near the 17-mile Auburndale checkpoint, Pawson took the lead from Johnny and ran alone through the hills of Newton. Johnny stubbornly pursued, hoping Pawson's beautiful, rhythmic stride might falter.

Unbeknownst to Johnny, Pat Dengis, the powerful, fast-finisher from Baltimore, was making a spectacular stretch run. Dengis, who had placed second to Johnny in '35, passed twelve men in the last 15 miles. Johnny tried to hold Dengis off, but with a mile to go Pat roared past, vainly chasing the tiring Leslie Pawson, who would claim his second laurel wreath. "Les ran a wonderful Marathon. He was just too strong. He got away from me and that was it. Pat Dengis— he was like DeMar—he wasn't terribly fast but he could go-go-go mile after mile."

Exeter Street was undergoing excavation that spring, so the runners had to finish over a bridge of planks. Clarence DeMar, now 50 years old, delighted the crowds by finishing seventh, just ahead of Gerard Cote, who had pushed Johnny so hard at North Medford. But the real story of this race was Pat Dengis, who had uncorked his furious bid too late. "Poor Pat wanted to win Boston so bad," Johnny recalls. "He'd run five marathons a year—and win four of them, but comes to Boston—he never could win Boston."

In 1938-39, over a seventeen-month period, Pat Dengis ran eleven full-distance marathons and won nine of them. The two he lost were both at Boston. Tall and talkative, Dengis was a transplanted Welshman who had led an adventurous life before coming to America. By the age of fourteen he had begun shipping out as a deckhand on WWI supply barges and later on tramp steamers, touring the world. Three times before his fifteenth birthday his ships were torpedoed by German "U" boats off the coast of Wales. Twice more he survived collisions at sea. In a Buenos Aires bar he was drugged and robbed, and woke up on a freight train rumbling through the pampas—the great open plains south of the Amazon River. Barefoot, starving, he hiked 300 miles back to Buenos Aires in three weeks.

Eventually, Dengis emigrated to the States, where he sought more conventional work, first in a Baltimore steel mill, then at the Glenn Martin Aircraft Company as an aeronautical toolmaker. Dengis never ran a step until he was 31 years old. Then, without Pat's knowledge, his shop foreman entered him in a one-mile run at a company picnic. "Pat weighed 192 pounds," Johnny says, "After that picnic, from then on he was a runner. He lost 55 pounds. He was a character. He'd write letters about all the top runners and Jerry Nason would print them in the *Globe*. He wrote about me once, 'Kelley's got a heart as big as a water bucket.' " Pat Dengis made a rapid rise to the top of the marathon heap. He won the brutal Yonkers Marathon three times, twice when it was the national championship. But even the national title somehow lacked the prestige of Boston. "Forget the national championship," Johnny says. "Boston was it. Boston was the one Pat wanted."

Training with Kelley
by Hal Higdon

Two weeks before the Boston Marathon in 1935, John Kelley met a half dozen other runners in Framingham to run the last 20 miles of the course as a final test. "It was a Sunday morning," recalls Kelley. "There was little traffic back in those days."

Among the group was Les Pawson, who would win Boston on three occasions. Pawson felt good, and soon he had sprinted ahead, arriving at the Boston Athletic Association's old club house on Exeter Street three minutes before the others.

"If they had run the Marathon that day, Pawson would have won it," says Kelley. "Two weeks later, he was 27th and I was first. He had pushed too hard in training. He admitted to me that he had blown it, but he just felt so good that day."

Kelley remembers the training that he and other marathoners did in the era between World Wars I and II. They ran long runs—but not as often as today's runners. They did interval training on cinder tracks—but they called the practice of alternating fast and slow quarter-miles, "ins and outs." They felt no qualms about taking days—or months—off.

According to Kelley: "Clarence DeMar, who won Boston seven times, once told me that you have to do 20-milers when training for the marathon, but the trick is not to do too many of them."

Kelley enjoyed all sports when growing up in a family with ten children in West Medford, Mass.: "I tried football, but almost got killed. I liked skating, but didn't care to play hockey. Baseball was fun, but track was my cup of tea. My basic training came from working as a caddy starting at age eleven. I walked all summer long with heavy golf bags in the White Mountains, and that got me in shape. I'd walk to and from school every day too."

As a miler at Medford and Arlington high schools, Kelley never broke 4:40 for the mile, a time today's marathoners often equal en route to running 26. But few among today's elite marathoners work full-time jobs, as did DeMar, Kelley and those running a half century ago. Kelley worked for 36 years in mechanical maintenance for the Boston Edison Electric Company, a job that required him to be on his feet eight hours a day. He refuses to use that as an excuse, however, saying, "I think it toughened me up, climbing and walking and stooping. When I began my run at night I was tired, but after a mile the tiredness went away."

Kelley ran his first marathon in 1928 at the age of 20, a race in Rhode Island from Woonsocket to Pawtucket and back on Saint Patrick's Day. With the leaders at the half-way turnaround, he faded to finish in well over three hours. One month later, he ran the Boston Marathon for the first time. "There wasn't enough time to recuperate," says Kelley. "With four miles to go, I was walking. A man came along and said he'd give me a ride to the finish, which I gladly took. I didn't run Boston again for four more years."

In 1932, Kelley started Boston, but failed to finish. He ran 3:03:56 the following year. He won the race in 1935 and 1945, placing second seven other years. He missed the marathon in 1968 because of a hernia operation and failed to finish in 1956. In 1991, he started Boston for the 60th time and claims he has no plans to stop.

His fastest marathon at Boston was 2:30 in 1943, but his most remarkable performance may have been in placing fourth at the National A.A.U. marathon championships over the diabolically difficult course in Yonkers, New York, in 1962. Kelley was 54, yet he ran 2:37:42.

During his early years as a road-racer, Kelley trained only three or four times a week. One of the most prestigious road races in that era was a Thanksgiving Day nine-miler in Berwick, Pennsylvania, where the winner received a diamond ring. After Thanksgiving, most runners would cease running until January. "Then we'd start training for Boston," Kelley explains.

"Years ago, we just ran anything. There was no set program, no schedule. We just ran to enjoy it. I averaged 35 or 40 miles a week. I don't think I ever ran over 60 miles a week in my life. Middlesex Fells Reservation in Medford was a wonderful place to train. There was a wooded area and we'd meet up there and change our clothes. The surface was sand and soft dirt, not too many stones. It was worth the effort to travel there. Then we'd go on the track and run quarter-mile sprints, and gradually I began to learn a little bit more about training.

"Years ago, you know, we didn't have any training systems—we just went out and ran. We first discovered ins and outs at a ten-mile team race at Caledonia Grove, where they had a Scotch Picnic. We had four teams, five men to a team, on this little 220-meter track. Each man ran a lap, and before you knew it, it was your turn again. We switched off for ten miles. Later, Les Pawson and I were at another race and Les said, 'I felt great today. I wonder if that Scotch Picnic had anything to do with it.' We were doing intervals and we didn't know it."

Most of Kelley's workouts during the week consisted of runs anywhere from five to nine miles, with trips to the track once or twice a week during the warm months. He would run longer only when preparing for Boston during the winter and early spring. His work schedule with Boston Edison required him to work through one weekend, with three days off the following weekend. Kelley utilized these three "free" days for some of his best training: "I'd come home Thursday night and have a big meal, but do no running. The next morning, Friday, I'd do my long run of two to two-and-a-half hours. Saturday, I'd take it easy, maybe two or three miles. Sunday, I'd run an hour and twenty minutes, then take Monday off. I'd run hard every other weekend. The schedule worked fine for me."

(Intuitively, Kelley had selected a pattern close to the "hard-easy" training systematized and popularized several decades later by University of Oregon track coach Bill Bowerman. The hard-easy pattern remains the secret of most successful training programs even today.)

"I always ran on the watch and didn't worry about mileage," Johnny says. "In 1947, two Finns came over to run Boston. I trained with them and they told me, before you begin your workout, walk at a fast pace for 300 or 400 yards, then jog at an easy pace and build up into the fast part of your workout. I've been following that pattern ever since.

"I never leave the door and run immediately. In the morning, I get up and do the kitchen chores. I clean out the dishwasher, set the table, make coffee, and go down to my studio to pick out what I wear. It's my way of warming up. I don't do any stretching."

But Kelley still does speed training, doing "pick-ups" of 50 yards on the road. "What have I got to lose?" he says when asked why a man of 84 would want to train in a style usually reserved for youngsters. He admits to having been blessed by very few injuries during his career. He enjoys running in snow, but is wary of icy patches on the road. He wears rubber pads in the heels of his shoes, but prefers racing in lightweight models, rather than heavier, more protective shoes. He swims for relaxation, has a massage once monthly, and regularly relaxes in the whirlpool at a nearby motel owned by a friend.

"I can run all day," says Kelley, "but I don't have the speed I once had. I try to do something every day, whether walking or swimming, and once I start to get ready for Boston, I'll take a long run every two or three weeks, the longest two-and-a-half hours the end of March, then coasting down to conserve my energy for the big push. Last year at Boston, I had to walk a bit, but I made it. It's amazing how much ground you can cover when you walk and run."

Kelley's time in 1991, his 60th Boston, was 5:42:54. He struggled across the line on a wet and chilly day long after everybody else in the field had finished—but despite where John Kelley finishes, marathoners follow in his footsteps, rather than the other way around.

Hal Higdon is a Senior Writer for *Runner's World* and author of *Boston, A Century of Running*. His best finish at Boston was fifth in 1964, but he placed 26th two years earlier, one place behind John Kelley, who was then 55. "It was a humbling experience," Higdon recalls.

Chapter 6
"WHAT TIME IS IT?"

Today, along with a check for tens of thousands of dollars, the winner of the Boston Marathon receives a Mercedes-Benz. In Johnny Kelley's time, Marathon winners either bummed rides or waited for a bus or trolley. "I never owned a car until I was 32 years old. To get to work I'd pick up the streetcar at the corner of Massachusetts Avenue and Wyman Terrace in Arlington." It was at this streetcar stop that Johnny first met Mary Knowles, a stenographer for Bird's Eye Frozen Foods. Mary and her family were living just one block from the Kelleys' Palmer Street address. "One day I heard someone come up behind me. I looked at her and I was impressed. After three or four days I finally said, 'What time is it?' That kinda broke the ice and we started sitting together on the streetcar and became acquainted. Now and then she'd make me a sandwich to take to work." Mary Knowles, 32, soon started accompanying the Kelley clan to Johnny's road races.

Because stronger runners continued to outmuscle Johnny in the latter miles of the Marathon, he decided to add five pounds to his slight physique. The '39 B.A.A. was also an Olympic tryout, so Johnny decided to skip the North Medford race and preserve his strength for the Marathon. Except for Clarence DeMar's, Johnny's five-year record at Boston was the best ever: one victory, two seconds, a third and a fifth. But once again the field was extremely deep.

'37 winner Walter Young had returned, along with defending champ Les Pawson. Pat Dengis had won four straight marathons since losing at Boston the previous April. And the mercurial Ellison Brown was back, claiming he'd make amends for his Olympic failure and two stale efforts at Boston.

1939 was one of the very few years that Johnny Kelley would not be a major factor in the outcome of the Boston Marathon. He was 5th at Wellesley but finished 13th, a rare absence from the top five. Over an incredible seventeen-year span, Johnny would fail to make the top five only twice! "I never could seem to get going," Johnny told reporters. "But no alibis. I was tempted to drop out a dozen times. I kept thinking of making a position in the Olympic tryout rankings. That kept me running."

This dark, rainy Patriots' Day belonged to Tarzan Brown. Walter Young gave chase as far as the first Newton hill, but from there Brown flew through the cold mist alone, pacing himself perfectly, eclipsing Les Pawson's six-year-old course record by nearly two minutes, lowering the standard to 2:28:51. The starting gun was fired that day by Walter A. Brown, a much-loved sportsman and promoter who would later found the Boston Celtics basketball team. Walter had inherited the starter's chore from his father, George Victory Brown, who was one of the B.A.A. officials who had seen the first Olympic marathon in 1896 and organized the Boston race a year later. Were it not for Walter Brown, Tarzan's amazing romp might

OVER HILL AND DALE FROM

never have happened. The bronze, well-muscled Narragansett, chronically unemployed, arrived at Hopkinton without the $1.00 entry fee. Walter Brown gave Tarzan the dollar. (To support his family, Brown sold both his winning medals from Boston for $75.00 each. Other former winners did the same.)

Once again, the laurel wreath had slipped away from Pat Dengis. He finished fourth, his only loss in a year. Dengis had brought a protégé with him, a 24-year-old novice named Don Heinicke. As a boy, along with his father and brother, Heinicke had been stricken with tuberculosis. He alone survived. Originally a promising baseball prospect, Heinicke saw that dream evaporate when he lost four fingers of his right hand in a printing-press accident. Running became a way for him to build up his damaged lungs and stay competitive. Heinicke shocked everyone, including himself, when he not only beat Pat at Boston but finished second overall. "Look at this," Dengis joked, "he bites the hand that feeds him!" (Dengis had paid some of Heinicke's travel expenses.)

Pat Dengis began another string of victories after Boston, winning five more full-distance marathons. On December 19th, the new streak, and Pat's adventurous life, ended.

"Since he worked at the Glenn Martin Aircraft Company," Johnny says, "he decided to learn how to fly a plane. His wife was very much against him doing this—in fact they had words that morning before he left the house. He always used to kiss her goodbye, but

HOPKINTON TO EXETER ST

he never did that morning. He and another fellow were killed in a plane crash." Johnny, Les Pawson and Tarzan Brown traveled to Baltimore to bid farewell to one of the greatest runners who never won Boston.

Though the Boston Marathon was always foremost on every working-class marathoner's calendar, there were many other events on the racing schedule. "One of my favorite races was a ten miler at the Brockton Fair," remembers Johnny. "We'd run laps on a horse track. It started at 6:30 in the evening and after three or four miles they'd put the lights on. It was kind of a wonderful race. I never could do anything in it. Les Pawson won it. Les and I had more hammer-and-tong battles than anybody in New England, I guess."

Who'll Be Second? -:- -:- *By Bob Coyne*

"It's true," says Pawson. "They used to come to John and I all the time and say, 'Whose turn is it to win next?' Especially in ten-mile races—we'd greet each other like long-lost relatives at the start, but the truth is we never did give any races away."

"Les used to say, if he went to a race and I was there, full of life, full of fun, he knew I'd give him a hard race. If he came in and I was kinda down in the dumps and not saying much, he knew I was off-form. There was real camaraderie in my youthful days," Johnny says wistfully. "There's none of that today. It was like a family. There'd always be a small scoff after the race—the runners today just don't have the laughs we did.

"Sometimes we'd run races after working all day! I remember punching the time clock and driving down to Providence for a ten miler at 6:30 at night. The guy that put it on, Les and I used to call him 'The Burglar.' He was kind of a shady character. I won a set of pearls once, so I says to The Burglar, 'Are these any good?'

"'Oh yes,' he says, 'very valuable.' So I got them home, and the tag read $1.65.

"Running cost us money. We had to spend money to go to races. For bigger races, we'd get money for gasoline—for expenses, maybe $20.00 or $25.00, but a lot of times you'd spend more than what they gave you by the time you got home. I went all the way to Pennsylvania once and only got $15.00. To try and save some money, a lot of us fellas would ride together and chip in for gas and meals at the hotel. I remember once we drove all the way to Halifax, Nova Scotia. There was five of us and we only got $50.00 for all of us. But it was all a labor of love. We didn't really care what it cost."

Most of these events did not require any entry fee. Instead, promoters and race directors approached local merchants for donations and sold ads in a race program to defray costs. "They did have good prizes at some of the races: diamond rings, record players, radios, silverware, suitcases. I won a flashlight once and I asked the guy, 'Where's the batteries?' He says, 'Come back next year.' I won 22 diamond rings and 118 watches. I gave every member of my family a watch. I remember one time Les and I tied at the finish of a race in Worcester. I couldn't hear him coming up behind me because of all the cheering from the crowd. He caught me and we finished in a dead heat. We flipped a coin to choose between two 21-jewel watches: a wrist watch and a pocket watch. I won, and took the wrist watch. We won everything but money.

"I ran a race in Montreal once and won a refrigerator. It was the craziest race I've ever run. Twenty-six miles in a ballpark; 118 times around the field! There was a band playing and fire broke out in the right field bleachers. The guy who organized it lost his shirt because he had rented the ballpark. Montreal had a farm team. They were on the road and I got to use Jackie Robinson's locker. I beat Cote by a lap or so and won the refrigerator. Tarzan Brown won a refrigerator once down in Bridgeport, Connecticut, but he lived out in the woods and had no electricity, so he sold it.

"All those things come back in memories, y'know. I have so many stories I tell my wife a different one every day. Kinda doctor 'em up a little bit but . . . I entertain her."

In 1940 the Boston Marathon was, once again, an Olympic qualifier and Johnny had dreams of winning a trip to Helsinki, Finland, the home of his hero Paavo Nurmi. The day before the race Johnny went to a movie to try and take his mind off the Marathon. "There was too much pressure. My telephone was ringing every five minutes. I couldn't sleep the night before."

1940 was even more hectic than usual. Johnny was preparing to walk down the aisle with Mary Knowles a week after the Olympic trial.

Record-holder Tarzan Brown had a very high stake in this year's race. Though he had won in '39, he had failed to compete at Yonkers, the second Olympic trial. The only way he could make the team would be to win this year's Marathon. After finishing thirteenth at Boston, Johnny had taken third at Yonkers. A win wasn't necessary for him, but a high placement was crucial.

Wanting to look spiffy at his upcoming wedding, Johnny arrived at Hopkinton with a very short haircut. When the other runners all kidded him about it, Johnny told them, "I had it cut this way so the laurel wreath will fit better."

Gerard Cote was the early leader, but by the halfway point he had slipped back to fifth. Johnny was in the first pack along with Tarzan Brown, Les Pawson and Scotty Rankine, a shoe cutter who was the Canadian national champion. Pawson and Brown dropped back, leaving Johnny and Rankine to maintain the hurried pace.

At 21 miles Rankine had the lead, but Johnny soon edged ahead. The crowd gave Johnny rousing ovations all along the way, but his lead would last only for a mile. Gerard Cote was climbing back into contention, steadily moving closer to the front. At one point, to get by a bottleneck of official cars, he had to jump from bumper to bumper. First Cote picked off Tarzan Brown, who would soon drop out with leg cramps, ending his Olympic bid. Then came Pawson, then compatriot Scotty Rankine. At 22 miles Cote accelerated past Johnny, on his way to a surprising record run. Coming down Exeter Street, the dapper little Canadian, who could only find work three hours a week as a newspaper distributor, waved and blew kisses to the crowd and still broke Tarzan Brown's year-old standard, crossing the line in 2:28:28.

Johnny once again displayed his courageous heart, holding on to second for the third time in seven years, buoyed by the fact that he had clinched a spot on the Olympic team. At Coolidge Corner, a man stepped out and handed Johnny a piece of maple sugar. "It really gave me a lift and helped me finish," Johnny says. The man with the maple sugar was none other than 1919 winner, Carl Linder, whose exploits Johnny had read about in that yellowed, week-old *Boston Globe* he'd found by the Mystic River when he was eleven years old.

Don Heinicke, putting on a belated rush like his late mentor Pat Dengis would have, took third. Les Pawson was fourth, joining Johnny and Heinicke on the Olympic squad. While the flamboyant Cote celebrated late into the night at the Stader Hotel, Johnny began contemplating his switch from bridesmaid to bridegroom.

On April 27th, at a small ceremony in St. Agnes' Church rectory in Arlington, Johnny married Mary Knowles. Father Grimes presided; Johnny's brother Matthew served as best man. After the reception the couple went off to honeymoon in New York. "We went to hear Guy Lombardo's Band and they played 'I Didn't Know What Time It Was' which sort of became our song, since the first thing I ever said to Mary was 'What time is it?' "

After their honeymoon, the couple moved in with Mary's mother in Arlington and Johnny began preparing for his second stab at the Olympics. But the trip to Helsinki was not to be. "In June, Hitler invaded Norway. It was all over the newspapers. July 1st the Games were cancelled. The war put a hammer on the whole thing."

His Olympic dream deferred, Johnny continued his relentless pursuit of a second Boston win. When asked why and how he kept coming back to a race that spurned him so many heartbreaking times, Johnny shrugs. "The Marathon was so big and so well-known—I loved it, I guess. I loved the publicity, the notoriety. The crowds were always wonderful to me."

Many runners would take some time off after the Yonkers Marathon, and resume serious training for Boston in January. "I never took much time off," Johnny says. "I'd always run three or four days a week. I liked the snow."

There was plenty of snow still on the ground in March when Johnny again ran the North Medford 20 miler. In fact, the snow—in the form of an iceball—nearly cost Johnny the race. A young prankster tagged him in the thigh and the soreness never really wore off throughout the race. Johnny ran side-by-side with Les Pawson for 16 miles before Pawson eased off the pace to calm a stomach cramp, and Johnny opened a 75-yard lead. Worried about expending too much energy with the Marathon just a month away, Johnny considered dropping out. But wanting to win one for his bride of almost a year, he continued, holding his lead the rest of the way to capture the race for the sixth time.

The Pawson-Kelley duel at North Medford was in some ways a preview of what would follow a month later at Boston. The chilly temperatures of March were replaced by oppressive heat, but again, after separating from the lead pack, Johnny and his good friend ran elbow-to-elbow, stride for stride, over the sunbaked course. "I hung back until around Newton Lower Falls," Les Pawson remembers. "There was four or five of 'em running together—Lou Gregory, Scotty Rankine, Gerry Cote and John, of course. I caught them there and when I went by I thought well, gee, now I'm gonna go by the pack and if I go by fast it'll discourage these guys, y'know. They'll think I'm still fresh. But lo and behold—the only one that went with me was John. He was right on my shoulder and he stayed there."

"When Les came by," Johnny told Jerry Nason after the race, "he was going to beat the band. For about 300 yards he put on terrific pressure. Then he settled down. He was the man to beat. I knew I had to hang on to him."

Cooling themselves with countless cups of water supplied by the

race officials who drew their vehicles alongside them, Johnny and Les ran in tandem from Wellesley into the hills, their shirts and trunks drenched and clinging to their slender bodies. Johnny grimly absorbed the punishment of each upgrade, keeping pace with Pawson's stylish, more powerful charge. The stretch from Boston College to Lake Street was where Johnny had faltered so many times before. Coming down off Heartbreak Hill, Pawson, two inches taller and twenty pounds heavier, began to edge away. Johnny ignored the ghosts of Marathons past and continued to dog his friendly rival. The gap widened but Johnny was tenacious, waiting for Pawson to flag. But the smooth-gaited "pride of Pawtucket" never did. Johnny turned the corner of Commonwealth and Exeter in time to see Pawson cross the line and win his third laurel wreath.

Forty-eight seconds later, Johnny came across. As always, William Kelley was there to greet his weary son. Johnny had run 2:31:26, his fastest time to date, and still come up second best. "He had the stuff," Johnny conceded, blinking away tears. "It's heart-breaking, but if I had to lose, I'm glad it was to Les."

Don Heinicke finished third, completing a sweep for the three men who had been selected for the 1940 Olympic team but had not been able to compete. Clarence DeMar grabbed a few headlines the next day, not because he finished a remarkable twentieth at the age of 53, but because he stopped along the route *twice* to swing a fist at onlookers who got too close. One actually asked him for an auto-graph during the race. Further down the course Mr. DeMarathon socked another well-intentioned admirer who threw water on his feet, thinking he was cooling them off. After the race DeMar said he would've broken three hours if he hadn't had to stop and spar with the spectators.

Four spots behind DeMar was another old-timer, 59-year-old, white-haired Bill Kennedy from Port Chester, New York. Known as "Bricklayer Bill," Kennedy had won the B.A.A. event in 1917 after stowing away on a Boston-bound freight train and sleeping the night before the race on a pool table in the city's South End. "Bill Kennedy was from the old, *old* school," Johnny says. "He was kind of a rough character. He chewed tobacco and all that. He went over with us on the *Manhattan* to see the Berlin Games."

"Bricklayer Bill" carried the memory of his long-ago victory with him always and returned to run Boston for many years, to renew his treasured friendships and to refresh his memory of that golden moment when he beat them all—even DeMar—and wore the laurel crown.

These days, on his solitary, early morning rambles on Cape Cod, Johnny Kelley sees very few people and even fewer automobiles, which is just the way he likes it. Those local motorists who do catch Johnny on the run, toot their horns as they pass, and the ancient marathoner usually responds with a wave. But those well-wishers who drive too close really get Johnny's Irish up. Too many near-misses over the years have made him especially sensitive to oncoming cars. "There was one time we were running in Medford and Les Pawson was on the outside—I was on the inside next to the curb of the road— and a truck was bearing down on us and I pulled him out of the way.

"Another time I've always felt very badly about—in October of '41 we went to run an 18-mile race from Salem to Lawrence. I was in the lead at about 7 or 8 miles and I heard a noise behind me—poor Les was struck by an automobile. The car went by me and he was stretched out all cut up—the bumper of the car hit his calf muscle and way in deep it caused a serious injury—it usta ache like a toothache. From that day on he was never really the same. He wasn't sure whether to go to that race or not because Yonkers was coming up about two weeks later, but—that's the way fate goes."

With reigning champ Les Pawson out of the running, the '42 Boston Marathon was really a toss-up. Johnny was of course listed among the favorites, along with Fred McGlone, a pipe-smoking railroad brakeman from Roxbury. Joe Smith, a milkman from Medford who'd won the '41 national championship at Yonkers, was entered, but he'd been sick earlier in the spring and arrived at Hopkinton with flu symptoms. A big hubbub was made about Tarzan Brown, who had missed the Wednesday deadline but was allowed to enter late because of his past accomplishments. The last time Brown had made an eleventh-hour appearance was in '39, when he crumbled the course record.

The day was tailor-made for marathoners: 44 degrees, cloudy and virtually windless. Walter Brown pointed his late father's ancient pistol skyward and fired. Johnny jockeyed for the lead with Fred McGlone and John Coleman, a young B.A.A. runner who'd won the North Medford 20 miler. When Coleman began racing at record pace, Johnny and McGlone followed. Tarzan Brown packed it in at 13 miles, dunking himself in the river at Newton Lower Falls before hitching a ride.

By the time Johnny, Coleman and McGlone hit the hills, they had just about killed each other off. "We faded badly," Johnny says. "But Joe Smith held back. He had a touch of a cold that day and wasn't even going to run, but his wife made him go." At 6 feet 2 and 160 pounds, Bernard Joseph Smith, the 27-year-old milkman, was easily the tallest, most powerful contender. But early on, worried about his conditioning, he ran conservatively, hoping merely to place high enough to help the North Medford Club capture the team prize. But as the race progressed, the sluggishness he had felt all morning began to wear off. Suddenly he felt superb.

Lou Gregory, a 40-year-old schoolmaster and national champ at 10, 20, and 30 kilometers, was the first to overtake the exhausted pacesetters. But Smith was biding his time, carefully stalking his prey. First he chopped down Johnny and Fred McGlone, who would finish fifth and seventh, respectively. Then he took Coleman, the early speedster who would call it quits just past Lake Street. Near Cleveland Circle, Smith burst by Lou Gregory, patting the smaller man on the shoulder the same way Johnny had greeted Tarzan Brown in '36. But Smith had more than enough moxie left to maintain his lead. He sailed down Commonwealth Ave., hurtling toward a new course record: 2:26:51. Gregory, too, would surpass Gerard Cote's 1940 mark.

Having seen Johnny's 1935 laurel wreath carefully mounted in a glass-covered case, Joe asked Johnny how he'd preserved it. "Wax," Johnny told him. Unfortunately, Joe used *hot* wax on his wreath, and the leaves fell off, leaving nothing but a thorny halo.

"Joe Smith was a big, strong runner," Johnny says. "He never did much after that, but that was his day. He owed it all to Isabel, his wife. She talked him into running. I remember a woman came up to Joe after the race and said, 'You should be off carrying a gun in the war.' That got him angry."

Just four months earlier, Japan had attacked Pearl Harbor, forcing the United States to declare war. Soon, Joe Smith, Johnny Kelley, and many other working-class marathoners would enter the armed forces. For the next few years the Boston Marathon's list of entrants would have a strong patriotic flavor as servicemen based in the States took leave and liberty to continue competing in Boston's annual rite of spring.

Though he was still running like a youngster, Johnny was nearing his 35th birthday. He had again failed to win his beloved Boston Marathon, but DeMar, Jimmy Henigan, and Les Pawson had all posted victories after turning 36, so why not Johnny? The quest continued. With the United States now fully engaged in World War II, it became more and more likely that Johnny would be called to serve, despite his age. All able-bodied men between 18 and 37 were eligible. In early June, while waiting for Uncle Sam's call, Johnny was struck a blow far worse than any last-mile loss in a footrace.

Johnny and his wife Mary had celebrated their second year of marriage a week after the '42 Marathon. They were still living in Arlington with Mary's mother, Celia Knowles, trying to save enough money to get a place of their own. "I was sitting in the living room on a Sunday listening to the radio when my mother-in-law called to me, 'Get the ambulance! Get the ambulance!' Mary was sick with cancer. There was no warning at all. She was only in the hospital for three days. The last words she said to me were, 'What time is it?' which were the first words I ever said to her at the streetcar stop. She died in my arms on June 6th."

"It was an awful shock to him," says Johnny's sister, Mary Donaldson. "He was devastated, but I think his running helped him."

"Johnny came down to run in Rhode Island a bit more after that," remembers Les Pawson. "He had running to take his mind off things."

"Running helped me get through it," Johnny agrees. "My running was good therapy, good medicine."

Chapter 7
"THE SMARTEST RACE I EVER RAN"

In November of '42 the call came from the U.S. Army. "I went down to the induction center and the guy looked at me and asked, 'Married?' 'She died,' I told him. He looked down over his glasses at me. 'But I'm okay, I'm doin' alright,' I said. Because of Mary's death they classified me 1B, which meant they could send me overseas any-time, but for starters I'd be stationed in the continental U.S. They sent me to Fort Devens, right here in Massachusetts, for about six weeks, then I landed in Fort McClellan, Alabama, in Special Services."

Johnny wasn't in the Army two weeks before he ran his first race as Private Kelley. He got a three-day furlough for Thanksgiving, which he used to compete in a nine-mile race in Berwick, Pennsylvania. He won the race for the first time in nine tries and was awarded a diamond ring, which he still wears on his pinkie. After a quick visit home, it was back to Fort Devens. "I used to run at night when we finished our training, and they usta say, 'What is it with this guy,' ya know, 'we've been crawling through the mud all day and everything and he's out running.' "

For the Kelley family of Arlington, the war meant saying good-bye to three sons; Eddie and Matt were both serving in the Pacific. Johnny was a faithful correspondent. His sister Mary saved many of his letters:

Well kid sister,

The Alabama sun is mighty powerful and I'm real tanned up and look like "Tarzan" Kelley.

I always look forward to the Boston newspapers and the Arlington Advocate Pa sends me. I enjoy reading about all the races so much. How are all my trophies, medals and scrapbooks? Are they dusty?

When I was at Mass last Sunday at St. Paul's Church in Birmingham I saw a most impressive sight. I was in the back of the church and a 55-year-old black man with both of his legs cut off at the knees hobbled all the way down the aisle to receive Holy Communion. It was something to see and impressed me very much as I've never seen such devotion like that before. He used his right hand to guide the way. Very touching!

Matty, Eddie and I will have plenty of experiences to talk about for the rest of our lives when this war is over. I worry about Matty and Eddie and write them often.

My main reason in writing is to ask if you would do me a favor? On or near the 23rd of May or any day before the 29th, could you please put some flowers on poor Mary's grave? I visited her grave when I was home for the Marathon. I know you will do this favor for me.

Write to me soon,
in haste and with love,
Johnny

In addition to the steady stream of letters he sent home to his family, Johnny also wrote to Barbara Raymond, a woman he'd met shortly before he left for Fort Devens. "There was a restaurant across the street from Boston Edison and I'd go in there to use the phone booth to call my mother. Barbara was in there having her lunch and she said, 'Calling your girlfriend?' I told her I didn't have a girlfriend. We started talking and she mentioned that she was from Acton, which was out in the country. I was lonesome so I wrote to her from Alabama."

Because so many runners were now in uniform, the '43 North

Medford 20 mile tuneup lacked some familiar names. Many enlisted men were saving their furloughs for Boston a month later. After a fourteen-month forced retirement, Leslie Pawson had resumed training and was returning to competition, a year and a half after being struck senseless by a car in the Salem to Lawrence race. His scarred leg still gave him trouble on runs of more than twenty miles, but it was time to test the waters. Now lead man on a crane crew at the Walsh Kaiser shipyard in Providence, Pawson, 38, ran away from Lou Gregory, beating the New York school principal by three minutes and breaking Johnny's course record for good measure. This startling comeback made Pawson the pre-race favorite in the Marathon.

In an effort by the B.A.A. to give war workers a chance to see the race, the '43 Marathon was held on Sunday, April 18th, instead of the traditional Patriots' Day, which was then always celebrated on the 19th. (These days, the Massachusetts holiday is observed on the third Monday in April.) Once again, the runners gathered at Tebeau's Farm. Since most of them hadn't seen each other for many months, there was a lot to catch up on as they were herded into the holding pen, a snow fence that was unrolled and set up so race officials could track the entrants and check the names off their list. Only 113 runners were entered, down from the usual 150-200.

Gerard Cote, now a sergeant in the Canadian Army, joined Private Kelley and a crowd of other soldiers and sailors at the start. 1942 champion Joe Smith was home on leave from Coast Guard duty, but decided not to compete. Major Walter Brown, who had fired the starting pistol since inheriting the task from his late father in 1938, now passed the antique gun on to his brother, George V. Brown Jr., who would handle the duty for the next 37 years.

The entire grind, from Hopkinton to the Hub, a head wind hit the runners flush in their faces. Les Pawson, wearing a jersey that had "Walsh Kaiser" across the chest, held the early lead passing through the six-mile Framingham checkpoint. Johnny and Gerard Cote were with him. Johnny sported a U.S. Army insignia on his shirt, while Cote displayed the Canadian Army's red maple leaf. From Framingham to Wellesley the trio pulled each other along. Cups of water passed from Cote to Kelley to Pawson as the friends ran three abreast.

Cote had injured his Achilles tendon a week earlier, when he stepped in a pothole while training. He ran carefully, avoiding bumps and holes in the road that might further damage his swollen ankle. Around Wellesley Square, Les Pawson fell off the pace, the effects of his long layoff starting to tell. Four miles later, at Auburndale, Cote led through the 17-mile checkpoint but Johnny trailed by only a step or two. Once again, Johnny found himself locked in a two-man struggle heading into the hills. Cote's wife, Lucille, riding in an official car, passed a bottle of cold tea to her husband, which he shared with his stubborn running mate. The wind continued to buffet their bodies.

Through the hills they dueled, thrilling the huge crowds that lined the course. The Gothic spires of Boston College loomed at the top of Heartbreak Hill. Cote still had a step on Johnny as they made the ascent, but Johnny eased ahead on the downslope. Commonwealth Avenue was then a trolley route. The tracks veered off at Lake Street, where the streetcars were stored in car barns. This day, Lake Street would be the end of the line for the fighting Irishman as well. Having been outsprinted by Johnny before, Cote decided to make an early bid, hoping his injured ankle would not betray him. He took the lead back and quickly opened a 20-yard gap that widened as Johnny weakened.

"At twenty-two miles," recalls Cote, now living in St. Rosalie, Quebec, "I was feeling well and I was running ahead. I gained a couple hundred yards more, a couple hundred yards more and I finish maybe a quarter-mile ahead of John Kellee." The pain in Cote's foot plagued him the final mile. "The only thing which save me is I was running on my left leg, just touching the ground with the right."

It was a courageous display by both runners. Cote's time was 2:28:25. Johnny docked an even 2:30:00, runner-up, now, for the fifth time. "Some of those second places were my own fault. But Cote—he was just so much stronger than I was. It was just his day."

Behind Johnny in third place was '42 national champ, Fred McGlone. Coast Guard coxswain Lloyd Bairstow was fourth. Les Pawson ran a highly respectable but personally disappointing fifth. After the race, Les made the decision to retire. "I liked racing, I liked to run," explains Pawson, "but I had a family, I was keeping a house. My heart wasn't in it same as before. I didn't have the fire and incentive to run like I did before."

Jerry Nason once wrote that "the physical and psychological contributions made to the Boston Marathon by Leslie Samuel Pawson should never be underestimated."

Les Pawson did quite a bit of running after his retirement from marathoning, but only sporadically. He stopped altogether for a period of about three years when he was in his fifties. It was Johnny, his longtime friend and rival, who convinced him to take it up again. If there is a tinge of regret in Pawson's reminiscing, it is in the fact that he did not continue training and racing after his prime competitive years. "That's where 'Old Kel' was smart," says Pawson. "He never stopped."

"Les said he didn't have the same incentive," Johnny says. "I *did*, you know."

After the race, Johnny returned to duty in Alabama. Four months later he was honorably discharged. "In August all men over 35 were allowed to leave the Army. I came home and went back to work at Boston Edison." At Edison, Johnny switched from security guard to maintenance man. He also renewed his acquaintance with Barbara Raymond, the woman he'd met just before entering the army. Barbara had worked at the Acton Machine Company during the war, then started breeding and raising boxer dogs. She and Johnny began dating, and soon decided to marry and settle in West Acton. The marriage would last a little more than six years. "She was a nice girl," Johnny says. "We just weren't compatible. All my life I've been a very impatient person and it's cost me dearly. Not only in running, but in a lot of other things too."

On September 6th, Johnny celebrated his 36th birthday by winning the National 20-kilometer race in Providence, Rhode Island. It was the second year in a row he'd won a national championship on his birthday. In November Johnny returned to Yonkers, a race he hadn't won since 1935. Yonkers was now the national championship. Though Boston was always the race Johnny desired most, a national marathon crown was one of the few A.A.U. distance titles he had not yet claimed. But Gerard Cote would win Yonkers for the second time in one of the most exciting races in Yonkers history. Little more than a minute separated the top four runners.

Though it would take Johnny fifteen years to win Yonkers again, he always enjoyed testing himself on this rugged course. At Yonkers, runners could easily expect to run five minutes or more slower than what they clocked at Boston. "The Chippewa Club that put that race on was wonderful," Johnny says. "They had water stops all the way along, but one time, at 23 miles—no more water. My mouth was like cotton. I'm dying for a drink. So from a side street comes this boy about sixteen years old with a white uniform on and a change purse around his waist, and a cart with Hoodsies and popsicles. I figured the good Lord must've sent this guy. I staggered over and said. 'Can I have a popsicle?'

" 'Oh sure,' he says. He took out a nice frozen orange popsicle. 'Where's your dime?' he says.

"I said, 'I have no money now! I'll pay you after the race.'

"He said, 'You cheap bastard!' And he put it back. I'm not makin' it up. Scout's honor.

"Then I went along another quarter-mile and—I can still see that little three-year-old girl with blond hair coming across the lawn. Her daddy sent her over with a great big, new sponge with ice-cold water. 'Here you are, mister.' With tears in my eyes I took the sponge. That's how I finished Yonkers that year.

"Gerry Cote would drink cold tea during the races an' he used to say, 'If I have my tea I win Yonkers,' ya know, with the French accent. Cote from 'Can-a-dar,' by gar! I have my tea, I win Yonkers. I beat 'John-nee Kellee.' He was a character, always full of laughs. He smoked cigars and a pipe, but they never bothered his training."

Mortal enemies on the roads, Johnny and the carefree Cote were otherwise fine friends. In fact, in 1944, prior to the Marathon, Johnny welcomed Cote to his home in West Acton one evening. A few days later they would battle each other again, this time in one of the most dramatic struggles ever staged at Boston. Because of the war, the field had shrunk to just 69 men. But only two runners really mattered that day. After the first fifteen miles, Cote set the pace alone, wondering where all the other runners were, especially 'John Kellee.' Trying a different strategy, Johnny was biding his time. At 17 miles, the people's choice was still sitting back in third, silently stalking Cote, who was cruising toward the Newton hills. By the time Cote hit the first incline, heading toward the Brae Burn Country Club, Johnny had taken over second place and had closed to within 100 yards. Cote maintained his lead over the hills, but

Johnny was confidently moving closer, showing unusual patience.

Down Heartbreak Hill, past Lake Street and through Cleveland Circle they went. Cote the fox, Johnny the relentless hound. Finally, on Beacon Street, Johnny pulled alongside Cote. For one mile they ran as a pair, then the battle began. They took turns hurling surges at each other, testing, probing. When Johnny reached for water, Cote marched ahead. Each time, Johnny rushed right back to Cote's shoulder. On through Kenmore Square they charged; less than one mile remained. Bostonians had never seen such a fierce finale.

With a mere 700 yards to go, Cote unleashed yet another challenge. This time the strain was too great. Johnny failed to answer and Cote edged away. Running on empty, Johnny's gigantic heart helped him maintain the pressure. In 1940, Cote had pranced down Exeter Street blowing kisses off the palm of his hand to the audience that lined the curbs. This time Cote was looking back over his shoulder as he hurried toward the tape, which he broke just 12 seconds ahead of Johnny. "I shed a tear afterwards," Johnny recalls, "I really cried—to see him go over the line—I could almost touch him."

You had to go back to 1906 to find a closer contest. This was now Johnny's *sixth* second place finish and the third time Cote had personally denied him the laurel crown. Of the half dozen heartbreaks, Canadians had turned Johnny away five times. Nevertheless, '44 was still a very successful running year for him. In September, he retained his National 25-kilometer title and was voted the A.A.U.'s New England Athlete of the Year. From Chicago, chairman Avery Brundage announced that John A. Kelley was a finalist for the James E. Sullivan Award, one of amateur athletics' most prized honors. (He would finish fifth in the balloting.) Had the war not cancelled the '44 Games, Johnny, at the peak of his abilities, almost certainly would have earned his third straight Olympic shield.

In 1945 the North Medford 20 miler was pushed back to May. Johnny shopped around for a few shorter tuneup races to take its place. A week before the 49th B.A.A., Johnny ran the Reddish A.A. ten-mile handicap race in Jamaica Plain. Because he was now 37 years old, the handicappers offered Johnny a 30-second head start, but he scoffed at the idea and took his usual place on the scratch line. Governor Maurice J. Tobin fired the gun and then toured the course in his limousine. Johnny came in second to sailor Charley Robbins, a

24-year-old phenom who had won the '44 national championship at Yonkers and finished third at Boston behind Cote and Johnny. But Robbins, probably the first college track man to take to the roads, had accepted a 30-second advance from the handicappers. Johnny bested Robbins for the overall time prize by 16 seconds.

Driving home after the race, Johnny's wife, Barbara, seemed uneasy. "It was April 12th, the day Roosevelt died. A mile from the house, she said, 'I've got something to tell you.' That morning, I must have been out of the house or something, my father had called and Barbara answered. A telegram had come from the War Department. I said, 'Why didn't you tell me before? I never would've run the foolish race.' I turned the car around and drove to Arlington.

"I got there and my father held up the telegram. 'Here it is,' he said. My youngest brother Eddie was missing in action in the Pacific. He was an Air Force tail gunner and photographer and they'd been flying a routine photographic mission over Japan in a B-29. The telegram didn't say if he was alive or dead, just missing. My father skipped the Marathon that year. He'd always been there to see me finish, but he called me and said he just wasn't up to it. He stayed home hoping he might get some news about Eddie."

Ninety runners answered the gun in '45, The inimitable Jerry Nason called this one "the event that certainly tries men's soles." Clarence DeMar was present, but instead of running he was reporting the race for the *Globe*. When Nason asked DeMar if he felt awkward working in the proof room for the *Herald* but writing for the *Globe*, DeMar replied, "Course not. You asked me to write; they didn't!"

Absent from this year's entry list was Sergeant Gerard Cote. Two years earlier, Cote had won Boston while representing the Canadian Army. He arrived home a hero and was featured by the Army in radio and newspaper ads endorsing victory bonds. But families of other servicemen complained that Cote was getting preferential treatment. The Army responded by telling Cote he could not compete in '44. But Cote, wanting to defend his title, took a leave from his duties as a trainer at St. Jerome, Quebec, discarded his military colors and ran in Boston as a private citizen, sponsored by a Montreal restaurateur. When news came of Cote's repeat victory, army officials in Ottawa were angered. As punishment, Cote was transferred to England.

A month earlier, Clarence DeMar had picked Johnny to win. "DeMar came up to me before the race," Johnny recalls. "He was writing it up for the paper—and he said to me, 'It's gonna take you a long time to warm up today'—to get going. I didn't know what he was talking about but he was right—I was 37 years old and I went out at a nice, easy-going pace. Leading up to Boston I really felt good that year. I'd gone out on a long run one Sunday and felt wonderful. I told my wife, 'If I feel this way at Boston, nobody's gonna beat me.' "

Coast Guardsman Clayton Farrar led the procession all the way into the dreaded hills. Johnny showed unprecedented patience as he followed in fifth, three minutes behind at Auburndale. Just before the 17-mile checkpoint, Johnny maneuvered ahead of Canadian Lloyd Evans and Charley Robbins, who, in later years, became known for running road races barefoot. Lloyd Bairstow, another Coast Guarder, was still in second. Farrar began to weaken on the second slope, then retired at the foot of Heartbreak Hill. Bairstow became the new leader, but he was far from being in the clubhouse. Johnny was beginning to move, tearing through the hills.

By the time he came down off Heartbreak, Johnny had shaved more than a minute from Bairstow's margin. "I paced it absolutely perfect. I could see Bairstow up ahead and it took the longest time for him to come back to me, but gradually I could see him coming back, slowly, slowly, slowly. With two and a half miles to go—at Coolidge Corner, I went by him. It was the smartest race I ever ran."

Once Johnny disposed of Bairstow, the celebration began. Stealing a scene from Gerard Cote's act, Johnny started tossing kisses to the crowd. "I shared my victory with the people of Boston. For ten long years they kept seeing me finish second, second, second, third, second . . . they rejoiced with me." Johnny wept as he coasted down Commonwealth Avenue. "There was a one-mile marker and I could barely see it, my eyes were so blurred from tears. I knew I had it won. I could've walked in. It was the most satisfying win I think I ever had, because it took me ten long years to win Boston again. It really was a thrilling thing."

DeMar wrote: "The best Marathon I ever saw! Shifting leadership; the favorite in the rear with a young, graceful runner in front; and finally two and a half miles of triumph!"

A decade earlier, race officials had arrived late to Exeter Street and there had been no tape for Johnny to break as he crossed the finish line. This time Johnny extended his chest and tore the tape with a joyous smile, finishing in 2:30:40.

Johnny's sister Marion remembers, "We were given a room in the Hotel Lenox overlooking the finish line, so we could watch out the window. It was a thrilling sight to see Johnny come in first."

After the race, Johnny sat on a cot and held court. He even sang harmony to *Sweet Adeline* with former Boston mayor John F. "HoneyFitz" Fitzgerald and Governor Tobin. After all the hoopla, Johnny headed for the family homestead in Arlington, happy to be able to give his worried parents something to take their minds off the unknown fate of their youngest son. Johnny wrote letters to Eddie and Matty about his victory, hoping both brothers would receive them.

On May 19th, the North Medford race was held. Though he had done little training since Boston and was troubled by the lack of news about Eddie, Johnny won North Medford for the seventh time. Jerry Nason, reporting the race, made mention of Johnny's distracted mood.

A few weeks later, a second letter arrived from the War Department. Staff Sgt. Edward Emmett Kelley was confirmed dead. "There had been a mechanical failure and Eddie had been sucked out of the tail blister into the ocean," Johnny explains. "The rest of the crew, eleven men, all made it back safely to their base on Saipan."

"The aircraft circled the area," wrote Lt. Col. P.B. McCarthy in his letter to William Kelley, "and after sighting the open parachute descending onto the water threw out a raft and radioed the position to the Navy which immediately sent out vessels to accomplish rescue. Dense haze restricted visibility although the crew observed considerable rough water where Sgt. Kelley was last seen . . . ."

Though there was a twelve-year age difference, Johnny and Eddie had been particularly close. "I remember the day he was born," Johnny says. "It was a cold, sunny day in February and I walked a couple miles over to the hospital at the Heights to see him and my mother. He was only about eight hours old. He was like the son I never had. He hung on me all the time, more than he did my father. I'd take him here and take him there."

"It's a strange thing. He had flown 13 missions over Tokyo and had been transferred to Florida for retraining. He was playing basketball and hurt his finger. He was walking along to go get his finger fixed and a four-star general's jeep stopped and picked him up. The general asked him how he liked his new assignment. Eddie said he liked it fine but that he wouldn't mind going back over to the Pacific if he could get some time off to see his family. Eddie came home on a ten-day furlough and then went back to the Pacific. He lost his life because he hurt his finger in a pickup game."

Not long after official word came of Eddie's death, the letter Johnny had written to his youngest brother describing his Boston victory was returned unopened.

BREAKING "BRIDE'S MAID"

JINX . . By Gene Mack

Strategically, 'Twas Kelley's Masterpiece Marathon Kelley Wins Second Marathon in 10 Years Boston Globe, April 20, 1945 by Jerry Nason

Somebody within his hearing at Hopkinton yesterday noon scoffingly remarked that, at 37 years of age, a little man known as Johnny Kelley was just cheating the rocking chair.

"Life," said John, grimly and to himself, "merely begins at 40 and I have three years to go. Let me at 'em!"

Two hours, 30 minutes, 40 1/5 seconds later he charged triumphantly up Exeter St., Boston, winner of the Boston A. A. Marathon race on the 10th anniversary of his original victory.

He did not stagger one solitary step of the way, which is 26 miles and 385 yards. He did not fret and fume, or worry his way over the macadam. He did not, in fact, do any of the things Kelley was supposed to do—including finishing second!

Kelley exploded like a buzz bomb from the fearsome Newton hills to the finish. At Wellesley, halfway down the course, he was a lamb, meekly marching along 750 yards from the lead. He was a lion at the finish . . . a lion who pounced upon the hapless Lloyd Bairstow of the Coast Guard at Coolidge Corner and tore both Lloyd and the Marathon stretch to ribbons.

Head Aided His Feet

Indeed, there was nothing about this fellow Kelley, who literally roared down the last long mile, that suggested a rocking chair had any excuse at all in his West Acton abode.

The entry who'd sold out for second place six times was invincible on yesterday's bright and brisk day . . . and he would have run until his legs were tattered stumps before he would have yielded to any man.

Strategically, it was his masterpiece.

Kelley has raced many Boston A.A. Marathons, 12 of them all told. Always he has raced them with all the stamina and speed and heart his little frame embraces. Yesterday he allowed his not inconsiderable intelligence to collaborate.

This time he did not pour all his strength into a wild attempt to gain a wide early margin on his pavement opposition . . . did not squander his running far back up the course where Clayton Farrar of the Coast Guard had so savagely set the pace.

This time Kelley was the master, held the whip in his hand . . . and he knew it. With clean, unpunctuated strides he bided his time down through Ashland, Framingham, Natick and Wellesley.

"I felt okay," said he, "but not wonderful. My legs weren't limber." At Auburndale he commenced to accentuate the positive. "Suddenly," he related, "I felt just dandy!"

Fifth at Auburndale

And at Auburndale, doorway to the Newton hills, Kelley was in fifth place. Nearly a half-mile out ahead the blue-trousered Farrar, showing a lot of early foot, was pounding along. And a quarter of a mile behind Farrar was another Coast Guardsman, Bairstow, 22, a native of Lawrence. And just ahead of Kelley were Lloyd Evans, the Canadian who'd clung to his side persistently, and sailorman Charley Robbins.

Nobody in the business can run over the craggy part of the course in Newton as can Kelley, the pony boy of the Marathon. He was like a string of firecrackers popping off. The first upward sweep toward Brae Burn Country Club ignited him. In an instant he'd flashed past Robbins, now Evans, and had set sail for the sea-faring men ahead.

Meantime, Farrar galloped grimly as far as his fuel lasted. And that was exhausted, along with Farrar, at the very bottom of Heartbreak Hill, the long, twisting, tortuous lift from Newton Center to B.C.

He stopped, staggered groggily around . . . and Bairstow came bounding past, full of run. Yeh, man! Bairstow was moving like a newsboy late for breakfast . . . but fast as he was, Kelley was faster. One minute and 15 seconds Kelley gained on Bairstow over the hills.

And as he hurled himself over the last one, at B.C., and set off down the long slope to Lake Street, he could, for the first time, see the faded blue shirt of Bairstow bobbing along 155 yards in front of him.

Ran Bairstow Down

Kelley got Bairstow in his sight . . . got a good bead on him and set out to run his man down. It took a good deal of running. Bairstow was buzzing along. Through Cleveland Circle they sped, and on down Beacon Street. Like a lion stalking his prey, Kelley stalked the Coast Guardsman. He inched closer and closer . . . and he was full of confidence, his stride sharp and clean.

Coolidge Corner is 23 miles along, three miles from home. Here, many a time and oft, Kelley had been a beaten man, sagging under the weight of the Marathon pressure. But not this time. This time Kelley was indomitable. And now he let go with his Sunday punch.

Galloping up to the corner, he laid spurt on spurt and Bairstow, although still strong and steady, came rushing back to Johnny. At exactly the intersection Johnny moved up to his man, and past him. Bairstow didn't have enough left to make a real fight of it. He had enough left to finish a good second, and no more. He knew it. Kelley knew it. The crowd knew it. So Lloyd, who did himself a considerable piece of running out there yesterday, just shrugged his shoulders and let Kelley go.

Boys, did Kelley go! He hummed down the highway. He was taking deliberate delight in tearing apart with his bare hands the "Haunted Mile" and all the rest of the tail end of the course that had beaten his body but never his spirit in many Marathons of the past.

Kelley was imbued with a new power. "It's the air in Acton," he said. "A Finn up that way says it's the best air in the country. That's why so many Finns live in that section."

Whatever it was, it sent Kelley coursing through Kenmore Square ("What a feeling to come over the bridge there and see nobody in sight. Hot damn!") and on into the home stretch like a runaway horse.

And that's the way he finished . . . won his second Marathon after 10 years of futile effort . . . full of fight and run.

You can take it from your Uncle Jerry: They have no immediate need for rocking chairs at the West Acton abode of 37-year-old John Adelbert Kelley.

Among Kelley's toughest opponents was a Narragansett Indian from Rhode Island named Ellison ``Tarzan'' Brown. Brown emerged from dire rural poverty to win a place on the 1936 Olympic marathon team, largely due to his 1936 Boston triumph, shown here. (Jerry Nason Collection)

Following his fifth place finish in the 1936 Boston Marathon, Johnny enjoys a song with (l-r) his mother Bertha and sisters Mary, Ruth, and Marion. Mrs. Kelley played the piano to wake her ten children some mornings. (*Boston Herald*)

Walter Young closes in on Johnny Kelley in 1937. (Walter Young Collection)

Inset: In 1936 Kelley traveled to Berlin, where he was the only American marathoner to finish the race, placing 18th. Here he is shown being led from the finish by Olympic officials clad in Nazi uniforms. (John Kelley Collection)

Pat Dengis is show with Kelley in the clubhouse of the North Medford Track Club shortly before the club's famed 20-mile road race in March 1937. (*Boston Globe*)

Bertha Kelley raised her marathon-winning son along with nine other children! (John Kelley Collection)

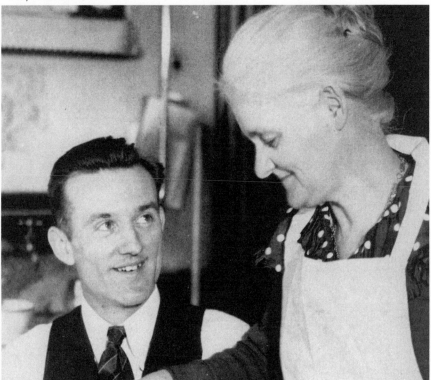

Les Pawson and Kelley are shown in the 1938 Boston Marathon, which Pawson won in 2:35:34—his second Boston triumph. Kelley finished in third place behind Pat Dengis in 2:37:34. (Les Pawson Collection)

The cream of American marathon running is pictured on the course at the 1938 Yonkers Marathon. From left they are
Gerard Cote, Ellison Brown, Les Pawson, Pat Dengis, John Kelley, and Walter Young. Ironically it was Dengis, who never won Boston, who beat this field of Boston winners for the 1938 national marathon championship. (Eve Dengis Bond)

Pat Dengis was probably the greatest marathoner never to win the Boston race. He is shown here winning the Yonkers Marathon in 1939 shortly before his premature death in a plane crash. (Eve Dengis Bond)

Inset: During World War II, Private John A. Kelley—shown here in 1942 in front of the family's Arlington home—joined his brothers Matt and Eddie in the service. In 1945, a week before the Boston Marathon, the Kelley family was informed that Eddie was missing in action in the Pacific. It was later learned that he was killed. (John Kelley Collection)

Gerard Cote leads Kelley in the 1943 Yonkers Marathon. 1932 Boston Marathon winner Paul deBruyn is seen handing water to the runners. (*Boston Globe*)

Following the 1944 Boston Marathon Kelley is shown celebrating Cote's victory with the winner. All told, Kelley finished second to Cote in three of the French Canadian's four Boston victories. (*Boston Herald*)

Neck and neck through Coolidge Corner, Kelley (r) and Gerard Cote rush toward the finish of the 1944 Boston Marathon. Both runners were even with 700 yards to go, but the superior strength of Cote allowed him to surge to a 12-second margin over his rival. (*Boston Herald*)

In 1945, at the age of 37, Kelley was one of the race's oldest winners. It had been ten years since his former Boston Marathon triumph. Kelley's time of 2:30:40 was bested only by his second place effort behind Gerard Cote in the 1943 Marathon, when he ran a 2:30 flat. (John Kelley Collection)

Chapter 8
"I'M GLAD YOU WON, STANLEY"

$\mathscr{T}$he 1946 Boston Marathon was the golden anniversary of the grand old race. Pre-race pundits thought sure this one would be a rematch between plucky Johnny Kelley and the suave snowshoer Gerard Cote, who had returned from duty in England. Tarzan Brown, who had not competed in the previous two Marathons or done much training over the preceding three years, was also back, courting the press, hoping to raise some eyebrows and secure a steady job. This uninhibited child of nature was living with his wife and four young children in a two-room, tar-paper shack in Charlestown, Rhode Island. A job might be in the offing, he thought, if he could run well and attract a crowd.

Another entrant actively seeking attention from the marathon scribes was Stylianos Kyriakides, a 36-year-old Greek distance champion. Kyriakides felt that by winning the Boston Marathon he could magnify the plight of his impoverished nation. During the Nazi occupation, Greece had been ravaged. Millions were starving, in urgent need of assistance. Though Kyriakides had a job as a bill collector for an Athens utility company, he wasn't much better off than those he was obliged to solicit. He had bartered everything he owned, including his home, in exchange for rations to feed his family. There were times when all he could provide them were a few scattered peas on each plate.

But Stylianos was a runner, good enough to place eleventh in the Olympic marathon in Berlin. In '38, just before the Germans invaded, he had traveled to Boston to compete. He dropped out at 21 miles, his soles covered with blisters. But he always remembered the Boston Marathon and the thousands of excited spectators who crowded the curbstones. Kyriakides went to his employers with a plan. If he could win the Boston Marathon, he might be able to appeal to the American people for aid. The Athens-Piraeus Electricity Company supplied him with extra food rations so he could train, and paid for his 5,000-mile journey to Boston.

This was the first year the runners dressed, not at Tebeau's farm house, but at Hopkinton Town Hall. (Later they would move again, to the local school gymnasium.) The Tebeaus now had fifteen children, and race officials thought displacing that big a brood for a day wasn't very practical. Having won the '45 race by laying off the early pace, Johnny sat back again. He was thirteenth at the six-mile Framingham checkpoint, ninth at Natick. At Wellesley he moved to sixth, next to Kyriakides. Approaching the legendary hills, Johnny took over second. The malnourished Greek, knowing Johnny was the man to beat, pursued.

Heading up Brae Burn hill, Johnny wrested the lead from Lou Gregory. Kyriakides—"Stanley" to the running friends he had made since his arrival in Boston—had no trouble keeping pace with Johnny through the hills. The Boston course was plotted to simulate somewhat the grueling route from Marathon to Athens at the 1896 Olympiad. The three Newton hills were much smaller versions of the torturous gauntlet of mountains—Hymettos, Paratha, and Stavros— just outside Athens which the dark-skinned, black-eyed messenger had traversed many times.

Johnny and the gaunt Athenian rushed through the hills, throwing short spurts of speed at each other, alternating the lead five or six times. Both cleared Heartbreak Hill with plenty of fight left. Johnny held a 20-yard lead at Lake Street. When he looked back it was hard for him to find Kyriakides, who was wending his way through a maze of official vehicles and seven jockeying press cars that spewed clouds of carbon monoxide everywhere. Indeed, both runners were so obscured by the blue, smoky fumes and maneuvering autos that many people lining the streets missed much of the dramatic fight.

Disappointed spectators booed and catcalled at the passing convoy.

From Cleveland Circle to Coolidge Corner Johnny put on another spurt that increased his lead to about 35 yards. But this final sprint was a mistake. "I made another boo boo," Johnny says. "I ran a broken pace—you can't run a broken pace in a 26-mile race but—when I got to Cleveland Circle I felt so good I said, 'I'm gonna leave this fella,' and I sprinted ahead. In about a quarter of a mile I was dead. I couldn't move."

In Kyriakides' right hand he clutched a small piece of paper given to him by his friend, State Representative George Demeter of Boston's Greek Council. Demeter, who owned the Hotel Minerva, was the man who annually lowered the laurel wreath on the head of the winner. In Greek, Demeter had written on one side "Do or Die!" The other side read, "We Are Victorious!" which is the message the Greek warrior, Pheidippides, is said to have uttered before dropping dead after running 25 miles from the plains of Marathon to Athens, in 490 B.C.

His black eyes smoldering like two hot coals, Kyriakides, carrying a desperate dispatch from his war-torn homeland, swept past Johnny with a mile and a half to go. "He just went right by me," Johnny says. "I could kick myself. I couldn't bide my time. If I had waited 'til I got to Kenmore Square or Massachusetts Ave., I think I could've come pretty close to getting it. I thought I could get away with it but there were four miles to go, and that's a long, long time. I've always been very, very impatient and I paid dearly for it. Somebody said to me after the race, 'I understand you let the Greek win.' I was out to win the race if I possibly could. There's too much work to hand it to somebody. He beat me."

The expected rematch between Johnny and Gerard Cote had never materialized. Cote arrived a remote third. Tarzan Brown, carrying too many extra pounds on his power-laden frame, finished 12th and was denied the soapbox he sought to try and gain a regular job, something he would never have his whole life.

"Does anyone here speak Greek?" called out one of the reporters after the race.

"I do," said Kyriakides. "But wouldn't it be easier if we all spoke English?

"I did my best for Greece," Kyriakides declared, sporting the laurel wreath George Demeter had placed on his brow. This modern-day Pheidippides had won the platform he needed to spread the word about the starvation that crippled his brave country.

Johnny listened to the horrible accounts of devastation, and tears of sympathy began to stream down his cheeks. "I'm glad you won, Stanley," Johnny said, sobbing. "I'm glad you won."

Representative Demeter sang Johnny's praises to the press. A week before the race, Demeter revealed, he had phoned Johnny and asked him for advice on a number of things. What kind of socks should Kyriakides wear? What kind of shoes? What should he eat? When should he taper off his training? Johnny willingly supplied the answers. "Kelley is the embodiment of American sportsmanship," Demeter exclaimed. "He doesn't get half enough credit for his unselfish spirit."

For several reasons. Jerry Nason proclaimed this race "the most significant Boston Marathon of all time." Most importantly, Kyriakides' pleas for help were answered. Americans immediately made generous donations to the relief drive. But the Greek's effort brought worldwide attention not only to his starving countrymen, but to the Boston Marathon itself. Soon, the 50-year-old footrace would grow from a largely domestic affair to an international event. Also, after seeing how congested and dangerous the Marathon route had become, B.A.A. president Walter Brown decided to limit the number of official vehicles on the course, dramatically improving conditions for the runners.

For the *seventh* time, John A. Kelley was a Marathon bridesmaid. "I've had a wonderful career and I'm not complaining, but with all due respect to the men that beat me, three of those seconds should have been firsts and the Greek is one of 'em. Walter Young is another one. People thought I was a running machine, but far too often I ran with my heart, not my head. If I only could have controlled my emotions I'd have been alright. A runner needs good sense *and* emotion. But it's water over the dam.

"All my life I've made a lot of mistakes instead of sitting down and thinking things through clearly. I should have tried to be a little more thoughtful. It's very sad but that's the way I was built. Even now I have to watch myself."

By now, younger, swifter runners like Charley Robbins, Tom

Crane, and Ted Vogel were beginning to give 39-year-old Johnny some serious competition, but he was still a powerful presence in New England road racing. In July, it took a freight train to stop Johnny. Literally. Pursuing from the scratch line in a ten miler in Somerville, Johnny and all but four other runners were held up around the three and a half mile mark by a slow freight. Springfield College runner Tom Crane, with a too-generous four-minute head start, plus the whistle stop, beat Johnny by only 18 seconds.

In autumn of '46, Gerard Cote "had his tea and won Yon*kers*," pulling away from Johnny on one of the final four laps around the quicksand oval at the Empire City Race Track, today called Yonkers Raceway. The national marathon title had gotten away again.

In '47, the Boston Marathon's upper echelon was dominated by foreign entries for the first time. Stylianos Kyriakides' victory in '46 had prompted the arrival of runners from around the globe, Kyriakides himself returned with two compatriots. Sevki Koru arrived from Turkey. The European champion, Mikko Hietanen of Finland, competed, as well as a trio of Guatemalans who were separated from their interpreter at the airport and dropped off at the B.A.A. by a bewildered taxi driver. A Korean contingent, partially sponsored by American GIs stationed there, featured Sohn Kee-chung, the '36 Olympic gold medalist, and bronze winner, Nam Seung-yong. (Both had been forced to represent Japan at Berlin under Japanese names.) The third member of their party was Yun Bok Suh, a 24-year-old university student. Hopkinton Town Hall was filled with the banter of foreign tongues.

For the American runners, this race was the first of three Olympic trials. The mantle of pre-race favorite had been lifted from Johnny's shoulders, but not the pressure of needing to produce a strong performance. Gerard Cote was back, as was milkman Joe Smith, entered for the first time since his record-setting run. '37 winner Walter Young also returned. But the times were suddenly changing. Americans and Canadians could no longer call this famed footrace their own.

B.A.A. president Walter Brown, after the preceding year's problems with official cars, reduced the number of vehicles to three. Two buses were employed, one for race officials, one for the press. A truck, outfitted with a special platform, carried all the photographers.

Yun Bok Suh, the least experienced of the three Koreans, survived a stern challenge from the Finn, Mikko Hietanen, to win the
race. Approaching Heartbreak Hill, the tiny runner, 5 foot 2, 115
pounds, lost contact with Hietanen when he was knocked to his
knees by a fox terrier. His knee bloodied and his shoelace snapped,
Bok Suh sprang to his feet, overtook the Finn on the famous
upgrade, and flew home to break Joe Smith's course record, lowering the mark to 2:25:39. The Finn maintained second place. The
B.A.A.'s own Ted Vogel, a 21-year-old from Watertown, attending
Tufts on the GI bill, was a surprising third. Gerard Cote was fourth.

Johnny ran poorly from the outset and was not among the top ten
at a single checkpoint. "I ran flat. I didn't have it," he said, after finishing thirteenth, only the second time in fourteen tries he had not
placed among the top ten. Still, he was third American, and in good
shape for the next leg of the Olympic trials.

At a Labor Day race in Littleton, a ten-mile handicap, Johnny
was introduced to a scrawny, 16-year-old high schooler from New
London, Connecticut. The boy's name was Johnny Kelley—Johnny J.
Kelley. This was the polite, blond-haired youth's first road race.
Amused by the appearance of a young runner with the same name,
Johnny offered the lad some words of encouragement, then waited
to be called to the scratch line. The schoolboy, who had traveled with
his father and a high school teammate eight hours by train and bus
from Connecticut, dropped out at seven miles. Johnny won yet
another time prize.

At Yonkers in October, Johnny ran seventh but was fifth
American, keeping himself in the Olympic hunt at the tender age of
40. Ted Vogel led during the early stages of that race, but by twenty
miles he had wilted and slipped back to eighth behind Johnny.
Barbara Kelley was following her husband in a car, providing him
with a special mixture of tea and honey. Barbara shared some of
Johnny's concoction with Vogel and it actually rejuvenated the young
runner, who not only passed Johnny, but caught back up to the leaders. With a terrific chase in the last half-mile on the raceway, Vogel
caught Torn Crane to win the national championship and the second
leg of the trials.

The '48 B.A.A. was the third and final tryout. Because it was an
Olympic year, most foreigners stayed home to participate in their

own trials or focus on preparing for London. This race would be a last hurrah for the old guard. Speedster Tom Crane and rising star Ted Vogel were expected to have at it, but Crane, who had won North Medford, self-destructed. Instead Vogel found himself contented with the cunning Gerard Cote.

The normally mild-mannered Vogel lost his temper during the race, claiming the crafty veteran was stepping on his heels and tossing water on his legs. He also charged Cote with crisscrossing in his path. Cote denial doing anything on purpose. "Vogel was getting ready to punch Gerry in the nose," says Johnny, who wisely elected to avoid any emotional front-running and maintain the steady pace he thought might clinch him a spot on the Olympic team.

Ultimately, the Canadian's ultra-distance training, some of it done in army boots, proved the difference. Vogel was doing most of his running on the track for Tufts, and was marathoning on a paltry 105 total miles of training since January. Cote left Vogel with three miles remaining, and won his fourth Boston Marathon by 44 seconds. After the race the combatants smoothed things out between them. "I couldn't have beaten him today anyway," Vogel conceded.

Unlike the impetuous warrior he had been in past years, Johnny Kelley kept to his plan. Remembering how his joust with Tarzan Brown in '36 had almost cost him a trip to Berlin, he ran cautiously throughout. After moving into eighth by Auburndale, he emerged from the hills in fourth and held that position all the way to Exeter Street, where Pa Kelley greeted him with outstretched arms. As the third American finisher, Johnny Kelley, at 40, was once again an Olympian. Another New Englander, Aulis "Ollie" Manninen, an assembly worker at a stove factory, was the third qualifier.

Gerard Cote's victory marked the end of a golden era. With their eleven wins in sixteen years, Johnny, Cote, Les Pawson, and Tarzan Brown, had raised the Boston Marathon to a new level of popularity. Their annual battles and distinct personalities had transformed the Marathon from a plodder's race into an exciting test that demanded speed and risk taking. With Les Pawson retired and Tarzan Brown prematurely so, only Cote and Kelley remained active. The free-spirited Quebecois would run his last Boston in 1955. Johnny, of course, would run on into infinity.

Chapter 9
OUR FLAG WAS STILL THERE

$\mathscr{D}$espite Johnny's renewed status as an Olympian, it was business as usual at Boston Edison. Though he was wearing the Edison Employees Club jersey at all his races, the company made no special concessions. "My supervisor said to the boss, 'This fella's going to the Olympics. He has no time to train.' Silence. He said it twice. Silence. That was the end of that. I really think they would've liked to help me out but they had company rules that applied to everybody. I understood that. All my Olympic training was done on my own time after work at night. To go to the Olympics I took my two weeks' vacation and some time off without pay, what they called 'pay deduct.'"

On July 1st, Johnny gave Ted Vogel a call; "Ted. You packed yet?"

"Packed?" said Vogel. "The boat doesn't leave for two weeks."

"I know. Not much time left, is there? I'm halfway through with my packing already."

Three days later, on Independence Day, the National 15K Championship was held in Fall River. It was at this race that Johnny again saw the young runner named John Kelley. Almost a year had passed since they had last met, and the 17-year-old was now a high school cross-country star. Along with George Terry, a teammate, the unknown harrier with the famous name challenged for the lead. When Terry fell back, young Kelley continued, running neck and neck with Vic Dyrgall of the Millrose A.A., an established racer. The neophyte wore flimsy track flats that quickly began to unravel. He continued to dog the leader, but soon the blisters came, then the blood. Still undaunted, he ran barefoot for a while before the pain forced him to drop out. Dyrgall went on to win the 15K title; Ted Vogel was second. The "real" Johnny Kelley took third in his last big race before the boat left for London.

The Olympic team left New York on July 14th aboard the *S.S. America*. On board was Marty Glickman, a former sprinter and one of Johnny's teammates at Berlin in '36. Glickman and Sam Stoller, the only Jews on the U.S. track squad, had been replaced on the 400-meter relay team by Ralph Metcalfe and Jesse Owens (allowing Owens to win his fourth gold medal), because Avery Brundage and the U.S. Olympic Committee didn't want to offend Hitler. Glickman was now a well-known sports broadcaster. "When he heard there was a Johnny Kelley on the boat he came looking for me," Johnny says. "He couldn't believe it was me. He thought it was going to be my son.

"One night all the athletes put on a talent show for the other passengers. Fortune Gordien was a discus thrower who did magic tricks. The women's swim and diving team put on a fashion show. The women gymnasts sang harmony and the men's team put on a skit. I sang 'Now Is The Hour' backed up by a twelve-piece band. Hildegarde—she was a famous singer—was one of the judges. She waved her hanky at me."

Other members of that '48 U.S. team were 17-year-old Bob Mathias, who would win a gold medal in the decathlon, and pole-vaulter Bob Richards, who later would appear on the front panel of boxes of Wheaties cereal. The Olympic village for the Games was the R.A.F. Academy in Uxbridge. The athletes slept on military cots in the flyers' barracks. Johnny shared a cramped room with Ted Vogel. Johnny's brother Jimmy went over to spectate and slept on the floor between the two marathoners. "We smuggled him in," Johnny says with a chuckle.

"England was still rebuilding after the war. They were a brave people and proud to have the Games," Johnny recalls. "Their economy was still very poor but they did a good job.

"I'm sorry I didn't get to meet him, but Zatopek competed in those Games. He won the 10,000 meters and just missed taking the

5,000." Emil Zatopek was a legendary Czech runner who, four years later, would make Olympic distance running history. "At Helsinki he won it all—the 5,000, the 10,000, and the marathon. All in eight days! It was the first marathon he'd ever run in his life! He had the ugliest, rocking-horse kind of shuffle you ever saw, but gee—boy, what he did was unbelievable. He was the best ever."

Johnny witnessed some magnificent performances. Fanny Blankers-Koen of Holland earned international headlines when she won four of the nine women's track and field events at London, and Harrison Dillard of the U.S. team shocked everyone with his performance in the 100-meter sprint. World-record holder in the 110-meter hurdles, Dillard had knocked down a hurdle in the U.S. trials, failing to qualify in his best event. He went to London as the third man on the 100-meter sprint team and upset three heavy favorites to win the gold.

On August 7, the final hot, humid day of the Games, the runners left Wembley Stadium to the cheers and applause of 82,000 spectators. The U.S. athletes had been issued the same sandpaper-like shirts that left Johnny's chest bloodied after the marathon in Berlin; this time he had brought his own nylon shirt with him. "I found a beautiful nurse who took the sash off the sandpaper shirt and put it on my nylon one."

The course was run largely on concrete roads through the English countryside. Because the times were very slow for such accomplished athletes, many were sure the course was long. Johnny Kelley, four weeks shy of his 41st birthday, finished twenty-first, in 2:51:56. "I knew I couldn't hope to win at London, but I did my best to represent my country."

Johnny's roommate, Ted Vogel, finished fourteenth. "Ted had an interesting thing happen to him in that marathon," recalls Johnny. "He was coming into the stadium and they were playing our national anthem. When he got to the finish line he was exhausted, but he stood at attention 'til the anthem was over. Then he collapsed. The London papers thought it was one of the highlights of the Games, very patriotic."

"It was an extraordinary experience," remembers Ted Vogel. "By mid-marathon I was holding on grimly, saying over and over to myself, 'Finish this thing. You have to live with it a long time.' As I ran through the tunnel under the stadium, I could hear my breathing echoing off the walls like a death rattle. When I came out of the tunnel onto the track, there was a tremendous wave of applause, then complete silence as I ran alone down the track.

"As I neared the end, they were raising the American flag and started playing the 'Star Spangled Banner.' Delfo Cabrera of Argentina had won the marathon about ten minutes before I finished, so, to keep things moving, they were staging a victory ceremony for decathlon winner Bob Mathias. When I got to the finish line no one was there, so I stopped and stood still. When the music was over, I passed out. To many in the stands it appeared that a young American, completely exhausted from the long, hot run, knew his 'flag was still there' and stood at attention for his national anthem. It was really instinctive, not a conscious decision."

After the closing ceremonies, many members of the U.S. team crossed the English Channel to France. "We saw the sights in Paris," Johnny says, winking. "We took young Vogel to the Folies Bergäre. He had the spyglasses all the time. Of course the girls in their costumes were beautiful. I couldn't get the glasses away."

From France, the track team traveled to Ireland. "I ran a three-mile race in Dublin against the Irish team on a grass horse track. They had Irish and American flags flying all the way around. I was supposed to compete in Belfast after that, but I got special permission to go with my father and brother Jim to County Wexford to see where my grandparents came from. We saw the schoolhouse in New Ross where my father's mother taught before she came to America."

After this brief pilgrimage, Johnny rejoined the team and made the seven-day steamship trip back to the States.

Chapter 10
MIDDLE-AGED MARATHONER

When Johnny got back from the Olympics, the entire New England running fraternity was all abuzz about a baby-faced schoolboy who had won both the time and place prizes at a ten-mile handicap race in Haverhill. The lad had gotten a five-minute head start and beaten Hawk Zamparelli, the scratch man, by seven minutes. It was John Joseph Kelley, the 17-year-old who had gone down in flames on the Fourth of July at Fall River.

At the Great Barrington Fair race, a ten miler on a clay horse track, both Johnny Kelleys appeared among the leaders list. The "real" Johnny Kelley finished second to Charley Robbins, who was now attending med school; the "new" John Kelley, unfazed by his more seasoned competition, came in fourth. As if one relentless Kelley weren't enough, opposing runners now had to contend with two!

"Many people think I'm his father," says Johnny "People still come up to me all the time and ask, 'How's your son?' He gets the same thing. 'How's your father?' We're no relation; we're just good friends."

To distinguish between the two in print or conversation, the running community began calling Johnny "Old Kel" or "Johnny the Elder." The fleet newcomer, of course, became "Young John" or "Kelley the Younger." "He's a wonderful runner in his own right," says Johnny. "He has a fantastic record." Indeed, the two Kelleys share more than a name.

Kelley the Younger would not make his serious Marathon debut for five more years, but once launched, he instantly became America's greatest marathon hope. He won the national championship at the rigorous Yonkers course an unprecedented *eight straight* times! Twice he was on the U.S. Olympic team. Competing at Boston year in, year out against some of the most formidable foreign competition ever gathered, Young John's record closely parallels that of his better known "forefather." His win in 1957 made him the first American to capture Boston since Johnny the Elder did it in 1945. Johnny's seven second place finishes are the B.A.A. record, but Young Kel was a B.A.A. bridesmaid five times. Young John has run thirty-four Boston Marathons so for, second only to Johnny's staggering sixty. The two Kelleys merged into one timeless hero in "Running," a poem by two-time Pulitzer Prize winner, Richard Wilbur:

> **Patriots' Day**
> **(Wellesley, Massachusetts)**
> *Restless that noble day, appeased by soft*
> *Drinks and tobacco, littering the grass*
> *While the flag snapped and brightened far aloft.*
> *We waited for the marathon to pass,*
> *We fathers and our little sons, let out*
> *Of school and office to be put to shame.*
> *Now from the street-side someone raised a shout,*
> *And into view the first small runners came.*
> *Dark in the glare, they seemed to thresh in place*
> *Like preening flies upon a window-sill.*
> *Yet gained and grew, and at a cruel pace*
> *Swept by us on their way to Heartbreak Hill —*
> *Legs driving, fists at port, clenched faces, men,*
> *And in amongst them, stamping on the sun,*
> *Our champion Kelley, who would win again,*
> *Rocked in his will, at rest within his run.*

In 1948, for the first time in thirteen years, the Yonkers Marathon wasn't held. Instead, to commemorate the golden anniversary of the annexation of the Bronx, Brooklyn, Queens, and Richmond to Manhattan to form Greater New York City, the national championship was contested elsewhere. The race started at Idlewild—now Kennedy—Airport and ended in Flushing Meadow Park. Race officials had gone all out for the event, receiving special permission from the A.A.U. to award prizes far more expensive than was usually allowed.

Still chasing his first national marathon title, Johnny made the trip a week after his 41st birthday. This was a true race of attrition. On this humid, 80-degree day, only 57 of the 108 starters completed the course. Johnny ran with Gerard Cote much of the way, but by 21 miles, Cote had fallen back. From there Johnny ran alone, the searing heat his only real challenger.

As he entered the stadium, Johnny waved joyfully to the estimated 40,000 applauding spectators who jammed the bleachers. Smiling broadly, he clasped his hands over his head like a triumphant prize fighter. He even managed a spirited sprint as he rushed over the line and breasted the tape. Ageless, persistent Johnny Kelley had finally won the national crown. His closest pursuer was Charley Robbins, who trailed by a whopping ten and a half minutes. "After twenty-two years of trying, I was very happy to win," Johnny recalls. "Television was just starting up around then and they gave me a TV set."

On March 27th, 1949, Johnny launched his twenty-third year of competitive running by winning the North Medford 20 miler for the eighth time. The B.A.A.'s Louis White, at the time one of the very few black distance runners in America, trailed Johnny by 250 yards. "Louis White was a great little guy," Johnny says. "He was from New York but he moved to Boston for a while to train. Everybody loved Louis." Just five feet and a quarter of an inch tall, but muscular at 120 pounds, Louis White was a well-traveled, bespectacled, Bohemian type. He was instantly accepted into the Boston running fraternity, but the Young Men's Christian Association on Huntington Avenue, where he was the Class C handball champion, would not rent Louis White a room.

In 1949, the venerable Boston Marathon was televised for the first time. A local station set up a single camera on Exeter Street and transmitted pictures of the finish. The flocks of foreign runners who had run Boston two years earlier were absent again. Americans and

Canadians reclaimed every top position—except the one they all prized most. The lone European entrant, Karl Gosta Leandersson of Sweden, ran the second half of the course completely alone, to win by three minutes over Vic Dyrgall. Johnny finished fourth behind diminutive Louis White, who celebrated his third place finish by playing handball at the Huntington Avenue "Y" the rest of the afternoon.

Less than one month later, the American trio of Dyrgall, Kelley, and White would battle each other again, this time for the national championship. The Yonkers Marathon was back after a one-year hiatus. But instead of the customary autumn date, the race was shifted to May 15th so it could also serve as the marathon trial for a trip to Norway and Sweden. The top two American finishers would earn the right to join the U.S. track team on a summer tour.

At a time when most marathoners have either retired or resigned themselves to the middle of the pack, Johrmy Kelley, at age 42, was defending his national marathon title. Vic Dyrgall, 28, an accountant for a New York chain store, was the favorite based on his second place finish at Boston and his A.A.U. victories at 15, 20, 25 and 30 kilometers. After twenty miles, Johnny and Drygall separated themselves from the pack. As a middle-aged marathoner, Johnny was now using his years of experience to stay near the top. No longer could he be tempted into dubious battle; he simply hung with his younger, faster opponent the rest of the way. In the last mile, however, Drygall's speed prevailed during a stirring stretch run, and he bested Johnny by less than a minute. Johnny had lost his national crown, but had won a trip to Scandinavia. After the race Dyrgall surprised everyone by announcing he wasn't interested in running another marathon that summer. Instead, third place finisher Louis White would make the trip with Johnny.

Just fifteen days later, Johnny, Louis White, and a few others ran their third marathon in six weeks! The Lawrence to the Sea marathon was second only to Yonkers in degree of difficulty. Starting at the common in the mill town of Lawrence, the arduous course traced through the Merrimac Valley to the beach in Salisbury. Hills abounded throughout. The longest, in Haverhill, near the New Hampshire border, was over a mile long. This was another race that Johnny had been unable to win, finishing fourth once and second three times.

An estimated 100,000 saw Johnny and little Louis White lead the field of 74 all the way to Salisbury Beach. When they reached the sun-scorched beach road, the pair were still side by side, Johnny's pale skin turning pink from the sun and strain, Louis' brown body glistening with sweat. "With about a quarter of a mile to go," Johnny recalls, "I could see they were drawing the tape across the finish line. There were three or four thousand people. I waited a little while longer, 'til I got about 200 yards from the finish—all of a sudden I got a jump on him—four or five yards. I gave it all I had and I won by two seconds."

As they broke the tape, Johnny and Louis White collapsed and fell onto each other and Jock Semple, coach of the B.A.A. "Louis says, 'What's the idea of running a marathon and tacking a 100-yard dash on the end of it?' " A graduate of NYU, Louis White was a free spirit who drifted from job to job, making just enough money to be able to live simply and pursue his many interests. Artistic and well-read, he had also been both a roller skater and speed skater on ice. For a while, he worked as a shipper at a beer warehouse. He also served as a part-time handyman at the Boston Arena, a job secured for him by Jock Semple, who longed for a member of his host club to someday win the Boston Marathon.

"What annoyed me during that Salisbury Beach race was that Semple was on the running board of a car, and he kept yelling at Louis," Johnny says. "This bothered me and it bothered Louis. Semple says, 'You better get going, Louis! You know what he's gonna do to ya!' He should have just kept his mouth shut."

When John Duncan Semple bled, he bled B.A.A. blue and gold. A veteran plodder and New England marathon champ who cracked the top ten at Boston nine times, he founded the B.A.A. running club after winning national championships for the Lynn YMCA and later for United Shoe Machinery in Beverly. It was while working at the "Shoe" that he met Sam Ritchings, the man who created the S.T.A.R. Streamlines. Jock served as the guinea pig for Ritchings' experimental designs.

A fiery Scotsman with a thick, sometimes confusing burr, Jock was, for decades, the guardian of the Boston Marathon. Serving as co-race director to Will Cloney, Jock handled thousands upon thousands of entries and inquiries from his "Salon de Rubdown," a phys-

iotherapy clinic he ran, first at the Boston Arena before fire
destroyed it, and later at the Boston Garden. He charged runners little or nothing for his services. Often feared because of his explosive
temper, Semple was frequently misunderstood by novice runners
who incurred his anger by crowding the entry table or lining up closer to the starting line than their abilities warranted. Rules were rules.

"Jock's enthusiasm would run away with him," says Johnny. "A lot
of people thought he was too gruff. I'd go up to his place for a soak
and a rubdown once in a while. He took care of all the Celtics and
Bruins players too. It was just a small place. He used to grill his
cheese sandwiches on the radiator. He wanted me to run for the
B.A.A., but he was too bossy. DeMar used to say, 'Self-directed work
is play,' and that's true. That's why I've always coached myself."

Jock Semple never did get Johnny to represent his B.A.A. running club, but he did finally see one of his own runners win the race.
In '57, as father confessor to Johnny Kelley the Younger, Jock saw his
prize pupil break the tape sporting the club's blue unicorn on his
chest, the only member of the host club to do so in the Marathon's
history. With Young John as the star, Jock's B.A.A. teams won numerous national titles.

Since Johnny had used most of his vacation time the previous
summer to go to the Olympics, Edison management was reluctant to
let him go to Scandinavia. Finally they relented, and Johnny got his
two weeks off in advance and a third week without pay Later that
summer, Johnny joined the fifty-three other members of the U.S.
track and field team for the flight from New York to Norway.

The marathon was run as the initial event of the first meet in
Oslo. Nine runners left Bislett Stadium accompanied by huge clus-
ters of bicyclists. Karl Gosta Leandersson, the Swede who had won
the Boston Marathon in April, trounced the field again. Johnny, little more than a month shy of his forty-second birthday, arrived
fourth. Louis White finished last, but was lifted by the cheering
throngs of Scandinavians, many of whom had never seen a black man
before. From Oslo the U.S. team moved on to Sweden. All told, the
team would compete in five different cities and towns. "After the
marathon, Louis and I had to earn our keep by rounding out the field
on the track. I ran the one mile and three mile and took a third and
a fourth." Johnny also placed third in a 25-kilometer race won by

Leandersson. Everywhere the team toured, Louis White was the crowd favorite, drawing cheers and applause even when opponents lapped him on the track.

"The trip to the Scandinavian countries was really another high point in my career," Johnny says. "It was always a thrill to represent my country. I owe an awful lot in this life to my running. I've seen the world!"

In 1950, another Korean contingent descended on the Boston Marathon. Led by 19-year-old schoolboy Kee Yong Ham, whom Jerry Nason quickly dubbed "Swift Premium," the Koreans swept the first three places. By this time, Johnny knew every bump and rock on the course and used his experience to finish fifth, the second American behind sailor John Lafferty.

Four weeks later Johnny was back at Yonkers, looking to regain his national championship. He hadn't won on the Yonkers course in fifteen years. Also on the line in this race was a trip to the Pan American Games in Argentina. This time, only one American would qualify to go.

Johnny tangled with Jesse Van Zant, a 27-year-old with excellent ten-mile speed and a third place in the '48 Boston Marathon to his credit. Born in Tennessee to a Costa Rican mother and a Dutch father, Van Zant came to Boston from California via New York. He was one of Jock Semple's top B.A.A. boys. The hilly course and the hot sun combined to stop more than half the field from finishing. Tom Crane held the lead at 22 miles, but from there Johnny and Van Zant, who had been running together for 15 miles, took command.

With two miles left, Johnny opened a 100-yard gap going up and over the final hill. On too many past occasions, Johnny had committed tactical errors that cost him. This time he received the benefit of a mistake by Van Zant, who let Johnny go ahead, thinking he could recover the distance in the final mile. Van Zant misjudged Johnny's staying power and could only reduce the margin to fifty yards. Rounding the Empire City trotters' track, Johnny poured it on, outlasting Van Zant by just eight seconds. His man simply outmaneuvered, Jock Semple was livid. After failing to win a national championship in twenty-two tries, 42-year-old Johnny Kelley had won the last two out of three, and was ready to pack for Buenos Aires.

Not long after Yonkers, A.A.U. officials announced that they

were going to send a women's team to Argentina along with the men.
To do this, however, the size of the men's team had to be reduced to
cut costs. Johnny was dropped from the team in favor of Jesse Van
Zant, who, it was decided, possessed enough speed to run the 10,000
meters as well as the marathon. To worsen the wound, Johnny found
out about it, not from an official phone call or telegram, but by reading it the newspaper.

"There was some funny business going on," Johnny says. "Semple
went down to New York and told them Van Zant could double up and
they bought it. I was the national champ and I'd beaten Van Zant, but
they knocked me out. Van Zant told me himself, 'I'm not in shape to
run another marathon.' He went to the Pan American Games and
finished seventh in the 10,000 and dropped out of the marathon."

Following the Games, the great Clarence DeMar wrote an acrid
letter to the *Globe:*

> *I note from a recent* Globe *that Jesse Van Zant, our U.S. repre-
> sentative in Argentina, finished the marathon in an ambulance.
> That is the usual and just climax to a phoney selection by ego-
> tistical autocrats who try to run amateur athletics. Johnny
> Kelley vanquished Van Zant in three of four straight marathons.
> Yet, by the usual shenanigans, Van Zant, as a younger and more
> docile commodity, for their vanity, was given the trip.*

"I really got the works," Johnny says. "It was a horrible disappointment"

Later that year, Johnny would suffer another personal disappointment. His marriage to Barbara Raymond ended.

Runners from around the world returned to Boston in 1951. A
four-man team from Japan joined a duo from China and the national champions of Greece and Turkey. For the second year in a row, a
19-year-old foreigner won the wreath. Shigeki Tanaka, born in
Hiroshima, won easily over career navy man John Lafferty, in
2:27:45. After getting treatment from an osteopath just two days
before the race, Johnny outran a sciatic nerve problem and finished
sixth, third American to cross the line. This was now the sixteenth
time he had arrived sixth or better, a solid addition to his amazing
record. But what made this race memorable, was that it was the first

and only time Johnny's mother came to see the Marathon.

"I was coming down off Heartbreak Hill toward Cleveland Circle and I saw someone step out from the crowd and wave a handkerchief at me." At the time, Johnny was running tenth. After he saw his mother, he caught four men before Exeter Street. "After the race we talked and I told her she should've been coming every year. She said, 'I think I've missed a lot, Johnny.'"

Not long after seeing her first Marathon, Bertha Kelley became ill with cancer. "She got very sick," Johnny remembers. "One day she got a call from my brother Jim. He was at work and had heard from a Major Cox. It turned out this fella was the pilot of the plane my brother Eddie fell from. Even though my mother was in pain, she wanted to meet him."

Major Omar Cox, visiting Boston from Texas, was reading the *Herald Traveler* and saw Jimmy Kelley's byline. He had never forgotten Sgt. Eddie Kelley, the good-natured young man who had vanished into the Pacific Ocean after being hurled from the tail blister of their B-29. He remembered that Eddie had talked about having a brother who was a newspaper reporter. Major Cox called the *Herald* and spoke to Jimmy Kelley.

Jimmy brought Major Cox over to the house and the Kelley clan gathered around and listened to him talk about Eddie. "He told us how well-liked Eddie was and filled in some details of the accident," Johnny says. Though seriously weakened by her illness, Bertha Kelley posed for a picture with the polite young man. "She sewed a button back on his coat for him," Johnny recalls. "She was very glad he took the time to look us up." Four days before Christmas, Bertha Kelley passed away.

Following his 1945 victory Kelley sang ``Sweet Adeline'' with Boston politicians (l) John F. ``HoneyFitz'' Fitzgerald, former Boston mayor and grandfather of President Kennedy and (r) Massachusetts Governor Maurice Tobin. (*Boston Herald*)

The 1946 Boston Marathon was one of the most hotly contested in the history of the event. Shown here are (l-r) Kelley with Stylianos Kyriakides and Charles Robbins. Note the paper in Kyriakides' left hand, inscribed on which were the words ``Do or Die'' on one side and Pheidippides' famed ``We are Victorious'' on the other. (*Boston Herald*)

Kyriakides checks his watch while crossing the finish line of the 1946 Boston Marathon where he defeated Kelley with a time of 2:29:27. (*Boston Herald*)

Kyriakides kisses Kelley after the race. Kyriakides became an international hero as his victory focused attention on a famine that plagued his countrymen in war-torn Greece. His victory both helped his nation and established Boston as a sporting event of international consequence. (*Boston Herald*)

Gerard Cote enjoys the spoils of victory following his 1948 Boston Marathon triumph, his fourth and final victory in the classic. Always a colorful character, he made the victory cigar a Boston tradition long before Red Auerbach. (*Boston Globe*)

Clarence DeMar shares the mantle of ``Mr. Boston Marathon'' with Johnny Kelley as a result of his seven victories. DeMar, like Kelley, continued to run the race well into his later years, finishing his last Boston Marathon in 1954, four years before his death at age 70.

Kelley is shown here winning the National A.A.U. Marathon Championship in 1948 at Flushing Meadow in New York. The 41-year-old veteran runner won in a time of 2:48:33. (AP/Wide World Photos)

Boston Athletic Association co-director Jock Semple (l) pins Kelley's 1961 Boston Marathon number on his singlet. Semple, an outstanding marathoner, was regarded as the heart and soul of the race, along with fellow BAA official Will Cloney, and Kelley. (*Boston Herald*)

Although they attended Arlington High at the same time, it was not until 1955 that Johnny met his future wife Laura Harlow at a performance of *Damn Yankees*. They married in 1957, with running colleague Les Pawson serving as Johnny's best man. (Nora Lewis)

John ``the Elder'' Kelley embraces John ``the Younger'' Kelley after the latter's victory in the 1957 Boston Marathon. Not only did they share the same name, but John J. Kelley finished second on five occasions, while his senior counterpart finished a bridesmaid seven times. (John Kelley Collection)

In 1969 Kelley was reunited with 1946 Boston Marathon Champion Stylianos Kyrakides (r). They are greeted by *Boston Globe* sports editor and marathon historian, Jerry Nason. (Jerry Nason Collection)

Painting was Kelley's chief hobby for over three decades. Here he is shown at his easel in the studio of his Cape Cod home. His paintings hang on the walls of countless runners, including such notables as Bill Rodgers and Marti Liquori. (*Boston Herald*)

Chapter 11
LAURA

$\mathcal{T}$hough there would be many more marathons, countless road races, and well over a hundred thousand miles of running ahead, Johnny Kelley's record up to 1953 was already phenomenal. He had won every New England A.A.U. championship from three miles up, and every national title from 15 kilometers to the marathon. At Boston that year, he added another top-ten finish to his credit, coming in seventh overall, second American behind Johnny Kelley the Younger who finished fifth in his Boston Marathon debut.

In that race, the foreign delegation manhandled the domestic talent. The winner was tiny Keizo Yamada of Japan. Just 5 foot 2 and 108 pounds, Yamada was literally blown down the course by a 25-knot tail wind. Chased all the way by Veikko Karvonen of Finland and former champ Karl Gosta Leandersson, Yamada obliterated Yun Bok Suh's record by nearly seven minutes, finishing in 2:18:51. The top four foreigners all broke 2:20.

Johnny's time of 2:32:46 was among his best His dark hair had begun its slow turn to a distinguished gray, and the competition was getting far faster and younger, but Johnny, then 46, wasn't conceding anything. His unrivaled record at Boston would eventually include eighteen top-ten finishes and twenty-five placements in the first twenty. Remarkably, the competitive flames still blazed and crackled within this aging warrior. The following year Clarence DeMar would run his thirty-third and final Boston; a year after that, Gerard Cote would retire, leaving Johnny as the last link to the glory days of the working class marathoner.

The Loneliness of the Long Distance Runner was not yet a popular short story and film, but that title best described Johnny Kelley in early 1955. Long divorced from Barbara, he was living with his widower father and his Uncle Pat, a lifelong bachelor, in the ten-room family homestead in Arlington. On April 16th, the Saturday before the Marathon, Johnny decided to go alone to a matinee at the Colonial Theatre in Boston. "It was *Damn Yankees* with Gwen Verdon," Johnny says. "I never would've gone to see that show if it hadn't been about baseball."

Johnny bought his ticket for $1.10 and went up to the second balcony. Seated in the same row with him were five or six women who attended matinees together regularly, always meeting for lunch before the show. The seat closest to Johnny was vacant, saved for a member of this circle who'd been delayed. Just before the curtain went up, the latecomer arrived and sat beside him. "It was my lucky day," Johnny declares. "The good Lord was looking out for me."

Laura Harlow was a career girl, an executive secretary to the vice president of the Kendall Company, a large manufacturer of health care supplies. She was late that day because her mother was ill and needed a ride home from the hospital. She wasn't sure, but the man seated next to her looked a lot like Johnny Kelley, the famous marathon runner who'd been a year ahead of her at Arlington High School. She hadn't seen him up close for twenty-seven years, except in newspaper photos and on Patriots' Day, when she and her parents would cheer the local favorite on as he hurried past them on Commonwealth Avenue. "Aren't you Johnny Kelley?" she asked.

Soon they were gabbing away. "In fact, my friends had to quiet us down finally," Laura remembers with a laugh, "Johnny says he remembered me from high school, but I don't think he really did. I remembered him. He was one of the top athletes who were adored by all the girls. I didn't know him that well. His brother Jimmy was in my class and Jimmy walked me home a couple of times, carried my books and things like that, but I never dated either one of them."

After *Damn Yankees,* Johnny asked Laura Harlow for her phone number and said he'd give her a call. On the eve of the Marathon,

Johnny phoned and visited with Laura and her parents at their home in Watertown. He left early to get a good night's sleep for the following day's 26-mile trek. It wasn't until after they'd been dating for several months that Johnny finally invited Laura to a road race. He'd been waiting, he said, for a really nice one.

The first race Laura Harlow attended with Johnny was the National 20K Championship in Needham, run in 90-degree heat on the Fourth of July. "John had me driving around the course giving him water. I was all dressed up in a pretty gypsy dress. I didn't know that I was going to be dripping water and sponges all over the place, hanging them out the window. My dress got soaked."

Accompanying Laura on her mission was the mother of one of Johnny's racing rivals, Tom Crane. "I was driving John's old Dodge coupe," Laura recalls, "which wasn't running too well at the time. After six miles, we ran out of water. Because it was a holiday, we couldn't find a gas station that was open. Finally I drove up to a fire station, and they refilled the pail for Mrs. Crane. They had a beautiful Dalmatian dog at the station and he jumped into the car and wanted to go with us! We had to push him out before we could go.

"By this time we had lost the runners. We tried to catch up to them, but I drove down a street and found it was a dead end. I tried to back up and turn around and the car wouldn't go in reverse! There were some fellows around there and we asked them to push us. So they pushed and got us going again.

"We drove on and came in after John had finished (sixth). So that was my first experience at a race. But I went back for more!" Laura laughs.

On September 21, 1957, with old friend Leslie Pawson as his best man, Johnny married Laura Harlow. "I'd be lost without her," Johnny said thirty-four years later. And he meant it. "Laura is very supportive. Without her help—she's been simply marvelous—packing my bag, cooking my meals, making sure I have everything. She goes to all the races and meets all the young crowd. I can't thank her enough for being so helpful in my career. Without her, I'm a nothing."

"Johnny says we make a good team. He's an extrovert and I'm an introvert," Laura explains. "We're opposites—absolutely. We balance each other out very well."

Since her inglorious debut at Needham, Laura has accompanied her famous husband to hundreds of races, from Hawaii to Japan, Bermuda to the Caribbean. "The trips have been wonderful," Laura says, "I've enjoyed it all, meeting all the runners and their wives and children. People have been very, very nice to us."

But all this globe-trotting wasn't something Laura had expected when she married the hometown hero. "Johnny's peak years were behind him, and I told him one time he could be sure I wasn't marrying him because of his running fame. Those days were all in the past. And that was very strange, because they weren't behind him at all.

"As far as I'm concerned, it's been a perfect life. I was over forty when we met and I didn't think I was ever going to be married. But all of a sudden Johnny came along, and we seemed to click it off— we say it was fate and I'm sure it was, really."

The first Boston Marathon Laura ever attended with Johnny was the last one he failed to finish. In 1956, after a poor winter of training, Johnny started out from Hopkinton on a bad leg, which worsened as he went along. After being passed by several runners he knew weren't of his caliber, he dropped out at Auburndale after seventeen miles. In the 35 years since, Johnny Kelley has finished every Boston Marathon he's started.

Johnny can count the injuries he's had on a few fingers. "Fifteen years ago I had a strained knee. But with ice and wet heat and rest, it went away. I've been very lucky. I was born with wonderful Achilles tendons." Except for a hernia in '68, Johnny's never been in a hospital. "Or a jail, either, " he adds.

Johnny shakes his head at all the injuries he reads about in running magazines. " 'Train sane.' That's my motto. All these runners that do 120 miles a week, they eventually run into trouble. Jeepers. They run every day. I believe that if you're tired you should take a day off."

In 1957, the Boston Marathon course was remeasured. Its length had been suspect since '53, when little Keizo Yamada cut dose to seven minutes off the record. But it wasn't until after the '56 race, when Antti Viskari of Finland lowered the mark to 2:14:14 and Johnny Kelley the Younger came across 19 seconds later, that officials decided to investigate. It was found that, over the years, road revisions, especially some in 1951, had shortened the course, forcing the start 1183 yards further back in Hopkinton.

1957 was the year Johnny the Younger ended a twelve-year drought by American runners. Running unchallenged for more than ten miles, the Connecticut school teacher, a B.A.A. unicorn on his chest, established the new course record in 2:20:05. Young John's mentor, Jock Semple, was beaming. B.A.A. president Walter Brown was practically overcome with joy.

Out on the course, Kelley the Elder, running thirteenth, got word of Young John's victory as he ran near Lake Street. Young John had spent the night before the race with Laura and Johnny in Watertown, as he would for the next twelve years or so. Choked up after the race, Old John couldn't have been happier if he had conquered the band of Finns, Japanese, and Koreans himself, "It was wonderful, just wonderful."

In June of 1958, Clarence Harrison DeMar, 70, died of cancer. Larger than life right to the end, DeMar had run a 30K race in South Hadley wearing a colostomy bag, a year before his demise. He worked until three days before he died.

Through the late '50s and early '60s, Old Johnny Kelley just kept rolling along, racing regularly, racking up several more top-twenty performances at Boston—no small feat given the now annual onslaught of foreign runners. His desire to compete was as great as ever, but Johnny began to look around for other activities. He and Laura were living with her mother in Watertown, just over the Belmont line. "I loved Laura's mother very much, but with two women in the house, I had to get out one night a week," he laughs. "So I took up woodworking."

Woodworking was a good diversion, but too much of a strain on the legs. "I'd work all day, then run, then rush to the Watertown Evening School for class. So I said, 'Next year, I'm gonna sit down,' I took up oil painting, which I always wanted to do. As a kid I could draw pretty well. I went two nights a week. Then Laura said, 'You should have professional guidance.' So I took lessons from Roger Curtis, a marine artist in Lexington. It was a wonderful association for eight years on Saturday mornings, which was a bad day for me because of races. But I went as often as I could. I also studied still life with Levon Matsakaunian in Watertown. We had a summer camp up in Maine, and I studied with Roger Deering of Kennebunkport."

After Laura and the Boston Marathon, oil painting is Johnny

Kelley's greatest love. He has been creating New England seascapes and snow scenes for more than thirty-three years. "It shows people I can do something else besides run. I really love the painting. As I've said, I'm a very impatient person, and it seems to me very strange that I didn't give it up. I do it year after year after year."

"I never would have believed that he'd stay with it," says Laura, "because he doesn't stay with other things that long. It means a lot to him."

For years, Johnny gave most of his artwork away to family and friends. Some became wedding presents for his many nephews and nieces. He still presents his paintings as gifts, but they have also become a source of supplemental income during retirement. "I've sold fifteen masterpieces so far this year, plus many, many others," Johnny says, reaching for a notebook he uses to track sales and expenses. "Runners come from all over the country to buy my work. My prices are fair but I've had to raise them a bit. My supplies have gone up terribly. I'd like to give more of them away but I can't. I'm no genius, but I'm no ham an' egger."

Because of his constant itch to be outdoors and on the move, Johnny paints only an hour and a half a day. His theories on rest and inactivity before running a race are contrary to conventional wisdom. "I discovered by trial and error that, if I have a race on Saturday, then the last day I'll paint will be Wednesday. Sitting down on Thursday and Friday, the inactivity throws me off. I ran a race one time and I couldn't figure out what was wrong with me. Then I realized I sat down for an hour and a half, two hours. Sitting down, you don't get any exercise. I could paint standing up but that would make my legs stiff."

Some canvasses Johnny puts on display are not for sale. "Fortunately or unfortunately, I never had any children. I'll never know. My running shoes and my paintings are the children I never had."

Kelley on Kelley
by John J. Kelley

In April, 1957, my wife and I spent a night as guests in Johnny A. Kelley's fiancée's Watertown, Massachusetts, home.

We slept undisturbed by those unnerving phone calls which we had come to dread on the eve of a Boston Marathon. Johnny had seen to that. The sole intrusion had come around 8 P.M. as we were finishing dessert.

Laura Harlow (soon to become Mrs. J. A. Kelley) rose to answer the call. "Let me take it," Johnny cut in, beating her to the hall table.

Then we heard his crisp, "No, he isn't. And if he were, I wouldn't tell you. He has a race to run tomorrow and you should respect the fact."

He shook his head angrily and rejoined us. "Kid," he addressed me, "someday you'll know, there's no worse combination in this world than ignorance and arrogance."

I already knew one thing: I had been admitted to the heart of Boston's King of the Road. And by a fillip of teasing fate, I bore the monarch's name, excepting middle initial.

1957 was fated to be my year at Boston. After my victory the following day, there would be no more laurel wreaths for me on Exeter Street, or, later, Boylston.

My namesake had won the Boston Marathon twice and placed second a record seven times. I would finish second a total of five times.

Pushing 50, Johnny A. remained a winner to his thousands of fans who braved the worst spring New England could deliver, just to witness his royal passage each Patriots' Day.

In the sports-crazed Hub whose plucky Irish he had come to symbolize, he might have won the mayor's seat for life.

"Go get 'em today, Kel," Oakley Country Club's early-bird golfers saluted him on the morning of April 20, 1957, as we limbered up in the rough an hour before motoring out to Hopkinton.

"Don't forget my 'son' here," Johnny yelled back, including me within the arch of his arm.

40th Birthday

I had met the man who was to be the prime mover of my marathoning life almost ten years earlier. The Littleton, Massachusetts 10-Mile Handicap Road Race of Labor Day, 1947, had been listed in the national A.A.U. Magazine's Calendar section. My high school pal George Terry had spotted the listing and decided the event would justify our sweet sixteen summer of pounding the back roads of our native New London, Connecticut.

(Time handicap road races, perhaps mercifully, have long since gone the way of the buffalo nickel, but in those days they were a staple of the region's road racing fare.)

Jouncing into Littleton in a crammed pickup truck which had been commissioned to ferry competitors from the local railroad station to the race's high school changing quarters, we sensed an extraordinary excitement in the air.

Labor Day, 1947 coincided with marathoner Johnny Kelley's 40th birthday, and he had chosen to celebrate by racing through Littleton's streets.

My own accompanying Pop was also in high spirits. "Of course, I've followed his career for years, boys," he told George and me. "How could I not know about a great athlete that owned the name I sign on all my checks, eh?"

George and I made our way into the musty gym.

That electricity haloing Littleton's honored visitor alerted us seconds before Pop led the chesty, bandy-legged celebrity into the dark corner where we were nervously laying out our racing gear on a bench.

Embarrassed by Pop's notorious habit of making fast friends of diverse charismatic strangers, I extended a tremulous paw for Johnny to shake.

"Yes sir, it's a great pleasure and honor to meet you," Pop was saying.

"Why, it's a great pleasure for me to meet all of you—especially a young fellow with my name who wants to run," Johnny nicely looped Pop's compliment my way. Then, to me and George, he said, "Good luck to you both today. Don't go out too fast"

He trotted about his business on those wondrous leprechaun legs, leaving me afloat on a cloud which, as things developed, would unload me ignominiously on a curbstone three miles short of the Littleton Ten-Mile Handicap's finish line.

In the race, I fell victim of hyperenthusiasm, inexperience, clobbering heat and humidity, and blister-inducing basketball sneakers.

By seven miles I was cooked. I gazed despondently at the stationary bloody stumps which only minutes before had been high-strutting feet.

Eventually a "meat wagon" scooped me up. It disgorged me in the midst of the race's exhausted but exuberant survivors on Littleton Green.

With a wrenching effort, I applauded the announcements of George's first-place finish and Johnny Kelley's time prize victory.

My bloody stumps begged for relief. I slumped against the comforting solidity of a massive oak tree. The ongoing awards ceremony clamor washed over me in sickening waves.

I wondered how I could steel myself for the dog-legged, 130-mile marathon, by train and bus, back to New London.

A hand touched my shoulder gently. I looked up into Pop's sympathetic face. "Say, Bud," he ventured, "you did all right for a tenderfoot—heh, heh."

"Oh Pop, no puns, please," I groaned. "I didn't even finish. I was awful."

Beyond Pop's hovering bulk, I saw George humbly withholding from me the huge silver loving cup he had won. And there was another figure behind George.

Pop tugged me by the wrists into a standing posture. "Are you going to congratulate these boys, Bud?" he prompted.

I fumbled for George's free hand. "Yeah, you did great," I managed. In that instant I recognized the rearward figure to be the famous Johnny Kelley. It advanced and clapped me affectionately on the shoulder.

"Hey, kid," Johnny said. "I dropped out of a few races too, you know, when I was your age, and, ahem, still do, every now and then. But you got some worthwhile experience here today. Next time, you'll go home with a trophy like George's, you'll see . . . "

Out of the corner of an eye, I could see Pop beaming.

Johnny appeared to be studying my nether extremities. He pronounced, "You'll make a fine distance runner. Yes, you've got a runner's legs."

My blisters were still throbbing as we all piled into Johnny's car for the ten-mile ride and the visit to his West Acton home. I still felt drained and disappointed by my ordeal.

But I carried an invisible trophy. I had only to think of it to know that my running life was going to turn out all right.

In addition to winning the Boston Marathon in 1957 and finishing second five times, John J. Kelley was a two-time U.S. Olympian and national champion eight straight times. A former schoolteacher, he is a freelance writer living in Mystic, Connecticut.

Chapter 12
"I'D RATHER RUN THAN RIDE"

$\mathcal{I}$n 1962, at the age of 54, Johnny ran his 32nd Boston Marathon, leaving him just one shy of Clarence DeMar's record. In with a record field of 301 starters, Johnny finished twenty-fifth in 2:44:36. At the same age, Mr. 'DeMarathon' had slowed to 2:54:14. A month later at Yonkers, a race he would run 29 times, Johnny would absolutely stun the experts and naysayers. On America's most punishing course, he ran 2:37:42 to finish fourth behind Young Kelley, Marine Lt. Alex Breckenridge and George Terry, Young John's high school teammate and brother-in-law. Largely for this magnificent effort, Johnny was named A.A.U. New England Athlete of the Year, an honor he had first won eighteen years earlier!

When he wasn't spending his weekends dogging the latest generation of runners or going to his painting class, Johnny was escaping to Maine. "We had a camp up there in Lyman, near Sanford. It was just a one-bedroom shack, but we had some very, very happy moments up there," he says, looking wistful. "It was on nine acres of land a quarter-mile off a dirt road. It cost $1,500.00. We had a fireplace, a wood stove, an outhouse—no conveniences. There was a pond and a well. I worked every other Sunday as a regular scheduled day. That gave me three days off the following week. I used to meet Laura at 4:30 at North Station on Thursday nights and we'd come home Sunday afternoon. I used to train up there all the time, early in the morning, and I'd see deer running. Those were some of the happiest times we ever had. Nothing but simplicity. But then people started breaking in all the time, and we finally sold it."

In the mid to late '60s, Johnny's beloved Boston Marathon was going through some changes. Race entries now topped 350, making the event more difficult to manage. Because its wealthy, worldly membership had declined drastically during the Depression, the B.A.A.'s magnificent, 5-story clubhouse, which once contained bowling alleys, tennis courts, an indoor running track and a Turkish bath, was closed back in 1936. Sold to Boston University and renamed the Soden Building, the old clubhouse continued to be Marathon headquarters on race day for more than twenty years. When the grand old building was razed in 1959, the B.A.A. took over two floors of the Hotel Lenox each Patriots' Day. But by 1964, that arrangement was no longer feasible. The race was getting too big and the runners were becoming a problem for hotel patrons.

In 1964, the Prudential Insurance Company was making plans to dedicate their new 54-story tower and adjacent complex on Boylston Street in Boston. Three days of special events were planned for the grand opening in April of '65. Searching for a culminating event on the third day, Prudential officials approached Marathon race director Will Cloney. "They wanted to know if the Marathon could be rerouted to finish in front of their new facility on Ring Road," remembers Cloney. "Since we were overrunning the Lenox, I said, 'Sure, as long as we can finish there in perpetuity.'" The partnership between the B.A.A. and Prudential lasted for sixteen years, with Prudential providing all sorts of volunteer help. "It was the smartest thing I ever did," says Cloney.

The start of the race in sleepy Hopkinton was moved back another 389 yards to the town green. The historical checkpoints, many located near train stops along the route, were preserved but adjusted. The traditional post-race bowl of beef stew would now be served in the Prudential cafeteria. None of these changes bothered Johnny Kelley, especially where the stew was served. "I ate it once," Johnny recalls, "after I dropped out in my first try, 1928. I got so sick I never touched it after that."

Neither the A.A.U. or the B.A.A. sanctioned it, but in 1966, the all-male barrier at Boston was broken. Jumping from behind a bunch of forsythia bushes into the race came the first female to complete the Marathon. Her request for an entry rejected by the B.A.A., Roberta Gibb, a 23-year-old Tufts graduate, ran anyway, and finished in 3 hours, 20 minutes, placing an unofficial 135th out of a record 415. In '67 she again ran without B.A.A. consent, but that day all the attention was focused on another woman, who ran more than an hour behind Bobbi Gibb. Twenty-year-old Kathrine Switzer had obtained an official number by listing herself as "K. Switzer" on the entry form and bypassing the physical exam by having her coach submit a health certificate.

Enraged when he saw number 261 pinned to the front of Switzer's sweat shirt, Jock Semple leapt off the press bus after her. Race director Will Cloney was actually first off the bus, but it was Jock who achieved instant infamy when he grabbed at Switzer's number and was sent flying to the side of the road by one of her escorts, her boyfriend, a burly college hammer thrower.

It would take until 1972 for women to gain official status in the Boston Marathon. Looking back on the efforts of pioneers like Roberta Gibb and Kathrine Switzer, Johnny can't believe how far women's distance running has come so quickly. "Joanie Benoit and all the rest, they amaze me! These days a girl will train for a couple of years and she'll run 2:40! I take my hat off to them. They even run when they're pregnant! How do they do it?"

Johnny finished ahead of both women on that cold, rainy day. Wearing a baseball cap and a Harvard cross-country jersey, a gift from the team and coach Bill McCurdy, with whom he'd been working out since 1954, Johnny came marching home in 3:13. "I was amazed the way the crowds stayed on in those awful conditions," he told Tom Fitzgerald of the *Globe*. "They gave me such a wonderful reception and every young fella who passed me had a nice word to say. It was almost enough to make you cry. It made it all worthwhile."

In '67 Johnny and Laura had a house built in Watertown. "It was practically on the ninth green at Oakley Country Club. I could step out my front door onto the golf course and do some grass training. They didn't object. As long as I stayed out of the sand traps!"

1967 was also the year Johnny turned sixty. He celebrated his birthday by running a marathon in Montreal. "I finished sixth in 2:50! Gerry Cote was there watching and he got so excited during the race he almost swallowed his cigar. Guess he thought I might win it," he chuckles.

In 1968, Johnny did something he hadn't done in thirty-six years—he did not compete in the Boston Marathon. "About a month before the Marathon I had a hernia operation and I couldn't run. March 13th," he says, displaying his incredible knack for remembering exact dates. "It was probably my age and all the heavy lifting at my job. The running, I suppose, aggravated it. I was in the hospital for a week. Nowadays, they take you in the morning and you come out in the afternoon."

For a while, Johnny considered wearing a truss. "Greg Rice, the two miler, wore one. He was in the middle of a race one time and it broke on him. He won anyway." But remembering how Tarzan Brown had collapsed after ignoring his hernia, Johnny decided to play it safe. "My doctor wanted me to start the race and go a few miles to keep my streak going, but my health is too important. I rode the press bus and saw Amby Burfoot win it."

Ambrose Burfoot was a tall, bespectacled 21-year-old psychology major at Wesleyan University. Now executive editor of *Runner's World* magazine, his running career has been a connective link in the history of New England runners in the Boston Marathon. His high school cross-country coach, at Fitch High in Groton, Connecticut, was '57 B.A.A. winner Johnny J. Kelley, the last American before Amby to win Boston. His roommate at Wesleyan in '68 was a talented, unassuming sophomore named Bill Rodgers, who, after moving to Massachusetts, became an eventual four-time winner of the Marathon and the first Boston area resident to triumph since Johnny Kelley in 1945.

Another Connecticut runner, Dr. Charley Robbins, was the first college student to compete seriously at Boston. (For most of the Marathon's early history the only collegians who braved the distance were pranksters and fraternity pledges doing it as a stunt.) But the rangy Burfoot was the first American college student to win the race. Fourth at Framingham, Burfoot was leading the record field of 890 by the ten-mile mark at Natick, but he was shadowed for many miles by Marine Lt. Bill Clark. Coming down off Heartbreak Hill, Burfoot finally began to open a small margin, which he maintained the rest of the way to the Prudential. Johnny watched the neck-and-neck battle from the back of the press bus, and motioned to Amby to maintain the pressure. Of the first Boston Marathon he had watched in over three decades, Johnny says, "It was a great race to watch, great to see Amby do it, but I'd rather run than ride."

By the early '70s, Johnny Kelley had already been a fixture on the U.S. running scene for forty years. He was a New England legend and well-known to the American road racing community at large. But that community was now growing. Distance running was already gaining favor before the '72 Olympics in Munich, but Frank Shorter's marathon victory, watched by millions of Americans on television, released the flood gates.

With *Love Story* author Erich Segal—a professor of Shorter's at Yale and a Boston Marathoner himself—commentating for ABC, Shorter rounded the track, the first American to win the Olympic marathon since Johnny Hayes in 1908. But an impostor had entered the stadium ahead of Shorter, stealing his deserved ovation. Segal helped to further crystallize the moment by vigorously condemning the impersonator, assuring those watching at home that Shorter was the true gold medalist. This moment, more than any other, is credited with igniting the running boom of the '70s and '80s.

In '72, Johnny was accorded a special honor. The Road Runners Club of America elected him into their Hall of Fame. Also inducted that year was Frederick Faller, the watchmaker who had advised Johnny during preparation for his Boston win in '35. A cross-country champion in his day, Fred Faller's A.A.U. record for ten miles had stood for 25 years.

1972 was also the year Johnny was preparing to retire, after 36 years with Boston Edison. He was retiring, it seemed, at just the right time. A new career, as a spokesman and goodwill ambassador for distance running and lifelong fitness, lay just ahead. Soon, running would become something of a religion for many Americans, and this white-haired man with the cherub cheeks was just the one to spread the gospel.

Johnny and Laura had been planning their retirement escape for several years. They would build a home on Cape Cod in East Dennis, a spot they'd visited many times and fallen in love with. Of course, running had something to do with their discovery of the area. For quite a few years, the town of Dennis held a celebratory weekend called Dennis Festival Days. Among the activities each year was a five-mile road race. By returning to this race year after year, Johnny and Laura had become firm friends with the Merchant family. Son Dwayne was a runner, but he was also a builder, just the man to construct Johnny Kelley's new home. On a wooded ridge, overlooking a pond inhabited by a family of swans, construction began. "We used to come down and watch the house in progress," Johnny recalls. "We'd stay at a motel and spend time at the site—change our clothes in the woods, go for walks, have a picnic. Laura would read while I went off to train."

Laura retired on September 1, 1972, after 29 years with the Kendall Company. Johnny left Edison four weeks later to the day. They moved into their cozy, custom-built ranch on October 25th, the day the house was completed. But what should have been a happy occasion was bittersweet. Three days earlier, Johnny's biggest fan, his father, had passed away at the age of 96.

Like his perpetually moving son, William Kelley believed that the secret to a long, healthy life was to stay active. He didn't run marathons, but he disdained the soft life so many retirees embrace. In his 80s he became the nation's oldest altar boy. Attending Mass one morning at the chapel of the Holy Ghost on Park Street in downtown Boston, he volunteered to assist a priest who lacked an altar boy. After that, for more than ten years, he was sacristan to the Paulist Fathers, working seven hours a day, six days a week, serving regularly as altar boy at the daily noon Mass.

William Kelley also spent as much time as possible outdoors, a practice Johnny adheres to faithfully. "Oh sure, I like to spend as much time as I can outdoors. My father was outdoors for 29 years as a mailman. Outdoors!" Johnny declares, punctuating his point by aiming a finger skyward. "Outdoors."

Ten months after Pa Kelley's passing, brother Jimmy, who had often cheered Johnny down the Marathon course while riding in a press car, also died. Jimmy Kelley had never fully recovered from injuries suffered when a fire destroyed his home in Belmont. Though the oldest of the Kelley siblings, Johnny was the only surviving son. "My four brothers are all gone now," he sighed. "There's not a day goes by that I don't think about them."

By 1973, the Boston Marathon's growing pains were increasing.

Fourteen hundred runners made the pilgrimage to Boston that year. In a vain effort to plug the dike, the B.A.A. had instituted qualifying standards. Chief among them was a rule that required all runners to complete any other A.A.U. sanctioned marathon in four hours or less. This time standard was soon lowered to three and a half hours, and later adjusted several times according to age and gender. But nothing could stop the flow. The boom was on. By the early '90s, official qualifiers would exceed nine thousand. "It really has been incredible," Johnny says. "In my day two hundred runners was a big field! Running was the working man's domain. We were looked down upon. People thought we were crazy. Now there's doctors, lawyers, male, female. Running used to be considered below the status of a professional person. Even President Bush does some jogging."

The '73 race was Johnny's 42nd Boston. It was also the source of one of Johnny's funniest running yarns. "Two days before the Marathon I had a muscle pull in my right calf. I started the race, but it tightened up on me right away. I stopped four times in the first mile to try and loosen the cramp, but it wouldn't ease up. I went over to a guy who was watching the race and asked him if he'd help me rub my calf. He didn't want anything to do with it. He told me, 'No, beat it.' "

Johnny kept running despite the pain. But a few miles further down the course, in Ashland, he limped off the road and collapsed in agony on the front lawn of the Stone family, who were outside watching the race pass by their house. Johnny picked the right lawn to collapse on. "It was the old Kelley luck," Johnny says. Sitting on the stone wall with his parents was young Jeff Stone, who happened to be the student trainer at Ashland High School. "He knew what to do. He sent his father into the house to get some Ben-Gay. The father was walking kinda slow. I'm saying to myself, Jeepers, could you hurry it up? I got 23 miles to go to get to Boston.'

"I'm dying, stretched out on the grass, and this lovely little girl, about ten years old, comes over and starts pouring cups of water on my head to cool me off. 'Thank you, dear,' I said. Then I'm lying there on my belly and this young trainer is doing a good job massaging my calf when all of a sudden two Doberman pinschers come running out of the house. When the father went to get the Ben-Gay he must've left the door open! The Dobermans started lapping my face and I'm saying, 'God help me, I'm gonna die.'

"They got the dogs off me, and the rubbing loosened my calf right up. I lost about six minutes, but I made it the rest of the way to Boston without stopping. Plus, I even ran ten seconds faster (3:35:02) than I did the year before.

"The people along the course are wonderful. One time I met a woman at a dinner and she said, 'I've always wanted to meet you.' I said 'Why?' She said, 'I live in Natick and I got married on Patriots' Day. My husband wouldn't come inside the church to marry me until you went by in the Marathon.'

"I got a million of 'em."

It didn't take Ol' Kel long to find new running trails around East Dennis, routes that are now well-worn after nearly twenty years of retirement. "I run every old place," he says. "In the woods, on the Dennis Pines golf course, down the back roads and bicycle paths, on the beach. I'm enjoying my running more so now than I ever did before. After punching a clock all those years it's great to do as you darn well please. I'm up every morning with the birds. I can't sleep. At my age all I need is five or six hours."

"It's still pitch black at the beginning of his run," Laura says. "I ask him not to go out while it's dark but he says, 'Well, I run under the street lights.' And he carries a flashlight with him. Some of his lady friends say, 'Don't you go by my house anymore?' " Laura teases.

Johnny smiles. "They say, 'Come in for a cup of coffee,' ya know. I don't want Laura to think I'm getting mash notes."

For several seasons Johnny worked out with the Dennis-Yarmouth High School cross-country team. With the coach's approval Johnny would sometimes get in a speed workout by running in meets with the junior varsity on the Dennis Pines golf course. The varsity harriers would start a few minutes before the JVs. Johnny would run it like a handicap race, occasionally catching some of the straggling varsity runners.

In August of '73, Johnny took Laura on a vacation to Hawaii. Johnny had heard that somewhere near Honolulu there was a memorial to the famous WWII correspondent Ernie Pyle. "Pyle got killed covering the war on April 18th, the day before I won the Marathon in '45. I always remembered that, so I told Laura I wanted to see the memorial." After visiting the Pyle Memorial, Johnny and Laura noticed a group of people gathered around another monument. They wandered over and learned that it was the "Courts of the Missing," elected to honor the 18,000 servicemen missing in action in World War II and the Korean War.

Once he realized what it was, Johnny anxiously scanned the names. "There it is, John!" Laura said. Listed at the top of one of the scrolls was 'Edward Emmett Kelley, Massachusetts.'

"I never knew it existed before," Johnny says, "The inscription says, 'Their resting place is known only to God.' I read that and started to cry."

It was several years after his retirement to the Cape that Johnny began what has been a long, proud association with the Massachusetts State Police. "During the mid-'70s, the State Police Striders conducted several major relay races from Cape Cod to Framingham," explains Sgt. Dan Donovan, himself a four-time finisher at Boston. "Johnny helped us out with some of those. We also sponsored a Junior Olympics program and Johnny was our honorary chairman. He's been a good friend to the State Police. He's one of only three people ever to have been made an honorary Colonel. The other two are John Wayne and Walter Cronkite.

"In '75, Johnny mentioned to me that he was having trouble getting into Hopkinton the day of the Marathon. The race was getting bigger and bigger and the roads to Hopkinton had to be blocked off early with ropes and barriers to control traffic. I've escorted Johnny in my State Trooper car every year since. I get him through the barriers, then, after he kisses Laura, I drive her into Boston.

"The Massachusetts State Police have a long history with the Boston Marathon," says Donovan. "If you look at some of the pictures Johnny has from 1935, you can see troopers on motorcycles escorting him to the finish line. Marathon detail is a matter of pride with us. It's a very prestigious assignment and we're proud to be associated with Johnny Kelley."

Sgt. Brian Greeley remembers two occasions when Johnny visited the Training Academy in Framingham. "We asked Johnny to come up and address our graduating class. He gave them a pep talk and ran with them. Our trainees were all about 6 foot 5, 250 pounds. They towered over Johnny, but he led the pack. Another time he came and stayed overnight with them in the barracks. He stayed up all night autographing their running shoes. He must've signed 200 shoes."

"They've been wonderful to me," Johnny says, pulling out his cache of State Police T-shirts, jackets and baseball caps. He even has a traditional 'Smokey the Bear' hat. "Everything but the cuffs," he laughs.

In 1975 the mystique of the Boston Marathon was further embellished by the unexpected record-breaking run of Bill Rodgers, a soft-spoken, unpretentious 27-year-old who was genuinely astonished after he erased Englishman Ron Hill's five-year-old mark. "This is absurd," Rodgers told Ernie Roberts of the *Globe*. "I can't run that fast. I must be dreaming the whole thing." En route to a 2:09:55 clocking, Rodgers stopped once on Heartbreak Hill to tie his shoe and four other times for water. "I can't run and drink at the same time," he said.

To the casual observer, Bill Rodgers' victory appeared to be a fairy tale, and it further fueled the burgeoning running boom. Rodgers was truly bewildered by his record run, but in fact, though he wasn't listed among the pre-race favorites, he had been running upwards of 140 miles a week, and was perfectly poised for his coming-out party. He would win three consecutive Boston Marathons in '78, '79 and '80, becoming nearly as identified with the event as Johnny Kelley himself. His popularity enabled him to launch a line of running clothes and open several successful running stores, both big taboos in Johnny Kelley's day.

"I remember once after I won the Marathon, a clothing store wanted to give me a new suit if I'd let them put my picture in the window." Johnny says. "I couldn't do it. The A.A.U. said if I did, I'd be a professional and lose my amateur status. Many people approached me and said, 'Why don't you open a sporting goods store?' Making any money off your name was strictly against the rules."

Now, of course, the line separating amateurs and professionals is totally blurred. The world's top runners command huge sums simply for showing up. Prize money and endorsement opportunities abound. "Running is big business now. Runners sign big contracts and run for a living. I don't begrudge Bill Rodgers and the rest of today's runners anything. Maybe I was born too soon, but I have no regrets. I'm rich in many other ways. Bill Rodgers deserves everything he gets. Bless him. He's been very good to me. It seems like he can't say enough good things about me."

Now in his forties, Bill Rodgers' own competitive career is winding down. Johnny Kelley is still his hero. "Though he's still known best here in Boston, Johnny's an international hero," says Rodgers. "Some people think someone like Jim Thorpe or Jesse Owens was the greatest athlete ever. For me it's Johnny Kelley. He's still doing it!"

The same year that Bill Rodgers began the introduction to his storybook career, the epilogue was written on the life of another Boston Marathon folk hero. Ellison 'Tarzan' Brown, 61, was run down by a van and killed in the parking lot of a bar in Westerly, Rhode Island. Despite several comeback attempts, the free-spirited Narragansett had never achieved his goal of snaring a third Boston win that he might parlay into a steady job. He was never able to lift his family from rural squalor. Two years before his death, Ellison Brown had been inducted into the American Indian Hall of Fame, joining such native Olympians as Jim Thorpe and Billy Mills. It was at a testimonial honoring this achievement that Johnny Kelley last saw his friendly rival and Olympic teammate. "Les Pawson and I went, and Tarz came over and put his arms around his two old competitors. It was a very nice reunion.

"Tarzan was a lovable character. He was just Tarzan, that's all. He was full of remarks that might come out of him like, 'Kelley boy, you gets in my way I'll run right over ya.' He was a great runner who should have been better, but he never did the proper training. He had so much power! I'll never forget his beautiful stride and untapped potential. It was a very sad ending. I'm very sorry about his demise."

Through the late '70s, the U.S. running boom continued its seemingly endless surge. Road races and running clubs were sprouting up across the country. Even Johnny Kelley broke one of his long-standing practices and not only joined a running club, but helped found it. "I'm a director of the Cape Cod Athletic Club," Johnny says. "I don't know what I direct, but we have meetings once a month and put on races. It's a good organization."

"If he isn't traveling somewhere, Johnny never misses a meeting," says Jack Glennon, Cape Cod AC president. "A lot of times the leprechaun in him comes out and he's really very funny. Running with the likes of Johnny Kelley is like playing baseball with Babe Ruth. I've run the Marathon with him a few times and when he makes the turn from Hereford Street on to Boylston, the applause and cheering could make you deaf. He takes his hat off and begins to wave it over his head and they go wild. It's incredible, really. Running with Johnny is a privilege. You're running with a legend."

In November of '77, Johnny appeared on the cover of *Runner's World* magazine. Shown waving to his legions of New England fans, Johnny's picture had the caption: "Will you look this alive on your 70th birthday?" The incomparable Kelley was still running Boston in well under four hours. After slipping down to the 3:40s in '78 and '79, Kel ran 3:35:21 in 1980, the year the National Track and Field Hall of Fame decided to waive their retirement rule and induct him. "I guess they thought I'd never retire," Johnny says. "They were right." Also enshrined that year were miler Jim Ryun and Olympic decathlon champion Bruce Jenner. Johnny was the first road racer to be so honored.

Ol' Kel, now 73 years young, was having a ball. He was already an oft-invited speaker at local schools and a prized guest at running club functions, but as he prepared for his golden anniversary at Boston, the very best times were just about to begin.

John A. Kelley
by Amby Burfoot

One of the many remarkable things about John Kelley is that some of the best days of my life have coincided with some of the worst of his life, and he has never held this against me. In particular, I'm thinking of the 1968 and 1991 Boston Marathons. The 1968 Boston had to be among John's worst—after all, it was the last one he didn't run. Due to John's hernia surgery earlier in the year, his doctors wouldn't let him enter. Of course, this didn't mean that John missed the Marathon. Hardly. It was too much a part of his blood. He would "participate" even if he couldn't run.

Indeed, I remember more of John that April than most others. Normally, he turns reclusive—almost crotchety—around Marathon time. He concentrates so hard on his upcoming race effort that he can barely tolerate any intrusions. Surely this "focus," as today's elite runners like to call it, is one of the underpinnings of his remarkable marathon record.

In 1968, since John couldn't compete, he seemed more relaxed and sociable than usual. On Marathon morning, I recall seeing him for the first time out in Hopkinton. He had ridden the officials' bus to the start to see and greet his many marathoning compatriots. Although I had known John only five years, it seemed much longer than that, no doubt due to the warmth and energy of his friendship.

That morning he greeted me as always—with a big grin on his face, a deep sparkle in his eyes, a bounce in his step, a wiry power in his grasp. Having John Kelley shake your hand is a special and memorable treat. He always shakes hands with both of his. First he'll reach out with his right hand to connect with yours. Then his left hand circles in on top. He pumps both his hands up and down so forcefully he nearly lifts himself off the ground. You can feel yourself being infused with his spirit and energy.

After pumping me with his handshake, John clapped me firmly on the back—he doesn't do anything half-heartedly—and wished me well. "Have a good race, Amby," he said. "I know you're ready."

I was very conscious that he hadn't used the most dreaded word: "win." John had been around too long and suffered too much under the weight of heavy expectations to fall into that trap. He understood, even as I did at the youthful age of 22, that you lose a hell of a lot more races than you win. His life seemed to prove that the best approach is simply to run down the road, one foot in front of the other, to discover where the footfalls will take you. Don't worry too much about winning.

That day turned out to be my day. I had never before felt so good in a race. For the first 20 miles, I ran almost effortlessly. By that point, Marine Lieutenant Bill Clark and I had pulled away from the field to wage a two-man battle for the laurel wreath.

Inevitably, the ease of the first twenty miles gave way to the torture of the last six. I pushed hard to escape from Clark on the Newton hills, but had no success. He was floating comfortably in my shadow. I sensed that my dreams of a Boston victory were slipping away. We crested Heartbreak Hill nearly side by side. Moments later, a big yellow bus rumbled by—the officials' bus. Jock Semple was leaning out the front door, yelling for me. "Give it hell down the hills," he roared, "Give it hell down the hills." Semple's blustery words renewed me.

Then the rear of the bus sailed past, and I received another boost, this one as quiet as Semple's was explosive. John Kelley was peering out one of the back windows, pumping his fists up and down, silently urging me to give it everything I had.

At this very point, in 1936, Tarzan Brown had passed John and run away to a Boston Marathon victory, scoring a win that John had badly wanted. In fact, famed Boston Marathon scribe Jerry Nason the next day described John's disappointment by coining the term "Heartbreak Hill." Ever since then, every Boston Marathoner has dreaded the long run up the last of the Newton hills.

Certainly, as I crested Heartbreak Hill in 1968, I felt on the edge of a major heartbreak. Clark was poised to surge past me. Instead, Jock Semple and John Kelley appeared, with their encouraging words and gestures. A moment later, Clark's footsteps faded into the distance.

I couldn't believe it. I was alone, at the front of the Boston Marathon, within striking distance of the finish line. My heart lightened and I looked up again. The bus was still within view. And I saw something I'll never forget for the rest of my life: John Kelley, still in the back window, still working both his fists, almost as physically and emotionally involved in the Marathon as when he runs it himself.

After I broke the tape at the Prudential Center, he was one of the first to reach me. He grabbed my right hand in both of his and pumped furiously. "Way to go, Amby," he kept saying. "Way to go. I knew you could do it."

It was memories of 1968 that made me walk out to the Boston Marathon finish line at 4:30 P.M. on April 20, 1991. I shouldn't have been there. I was supposed to be in my hotel room writing a Marathon story under deadline pressures.

At the same time, I knew John was out on the course running his 60th Boston Marathon, and I figured he must be having a bad day. He has come to hate the cold and damp. Sitting in my room, I remembered, of course, how much he had meant to me in my 1968 victory. I wanted to be there in the same way for him.

So I gathered up a friend and walked down Boylston St. to stand in the cold, dark and wet.

We stood there for a long time, with a handful of Marathon officials and perhaps fifty diehard John Kelley fans. John had hoped to run five hours, but the conditions were obviously slowing him. A few of those around us began to question if he would make it.

I couldn't resist turning to them. "He'll make it," I said. "He might run slow, but he'll make it. He knows that finishing is the only thing that's really important and, believe me, he's a finisher."

Eventually John made the corner onto Boylston St. We saw the police car with flashing lights first, then the duster of runners around John. He had his own little entourage, and the truth is, it wasn't moving very fast. But it was moving. Slow but sure . . . over the years, those have practically become John's bywords.

At last we were able to make out John's figure, hunched over, eyes down to make sure he wouldn't trip over anything, legs barely lifting. I could tell he was struggling because John has always loved playing to the crowds. On his best days, he'd finish the Boston Marathon weaving from one side of the street to the other to acknowledge the loudest cheers. He'd blow kisses to every young woman he saw. He'd lift his arms like an Olympic champion about to win a gold medal.

In other runners, I'd consider this behavior unseemly. I guess I've always believed in the loneliness of the long-distance runner—that we should be running for ourselves, not for the applause-meter. But when it came to John, I could only smile and clap all the louder myself. This was no Hollywood star who lived for the limelight. This was a simple man, a simple runner, expressing himself in ways that came naturally to him and enjoying every minute of it.

At the end of the 1991 Boston Marathon, however, John had no energy to play to the crowds. He was too damn tired. We responded anyway. I stamped on the wooden bleachers, clapped furiously, and yelled as loud as I could. I doubt John heard me; there was too much else going on. But here's what I was yelling. "Way to go, Kel. Way to go. I knew you could do it."

This was John's toughest and slowest Boston Marathon. But he seemed to recover quickly from the ordeal, just as he has from the other hard days in his life.

When I look back now over John's remarkable life, it is this—his resilience, his ability to always keep moving forward—that strikes me as the secret of his success. Not his diet. Not his training techniques. Not his genetic gifts. No, the key is that John never looks back.

Let us not forget: he has finished second at Boston seven times. He gave the heartache to Heartbreak Hill. He has won no prize money and collected no Olympic medals in the sport, marathoning, that he has mastered like no other. A lesser man would find plenty to grieve over.

Not John Kelley. He chooses instead to rise before the sun, to lace on his running shoes, to push open the door, to begin shuffling forward. He has run tens and tens of thousands of miles before this one, and it would be easy to relive them, perhaps to lament a few that didn't end well.

But this thought seems never to occur to John. He just keeps moving forward, knowing implicitly that the most important miles of his life aren't the ones behind him but the one he is running right now. And the next one.

Amby Burfoot, who first met John A. Kelley in 1964 and first ran the Boston Marathon in 1965, is today the executive editor of *Runner's World* magazine.

1981—Johnny's 50th Boston Marathon. (*Boston Herald*)

The royalty of New England marathoning gathered in 1983 to pay tribute to Les Pawson at a testimonial dinner. Pawson is show at the far left with (l-r) Johnny ``the Elder'' Kelley, John ``the Younger'' Kelley, Amby Burfoot, and Bill Rodgers. Eleven Boston Marathon victories are represented by this group. (Les Pawson Collection)

Kelley is shown in front of Faneuil Hall in Boston with the 1948 Olympic torch. He had been a member of three Olympic teams as a marathoner in 1936, '40, and '48. Joining him for the torch run are fellow Boston Olympians Tina Noyes (l) and Hilary Smart (r). (*Boston Herald*)

Former Boston Marathon Champions (l-r) Les Pawson, Gerard Cote, and Johnny Kelley are shown running in 1985 at the taping of the Emmy Award-winning documentary entitled *That Golden Distance* (Nora Lewis) in the same formation in which they ran in the companion photograph (*below*) of the 1943 Boston Marathon. (*Boston Herald*)

Kelley, shown here at a Cerebral Palsy fundraiser in the late 1970s, was a tireless supporter of charitable causes, particularly those which benefited children in need. (John Kelley Collection)

Johnny Kelley with some of his trophies in his Cape Cod home. Kelley gave away almost all his awards as he got older, some of which were refurbished and used again as prizes for road races. (*Boston Herald*)

Flanked by fellow Marathon winners Ibrahim Hussein (l) and Bill Rodgers (r), Kelley cele-brates the unveiling of the statue of his younger and older selves triumphantly crossing the finish line. (The Sports Museum Collection)

In 1996, Johnny Kelley received an honorary degree from Boston University. (*Boston Herald*)

Two symbols of the affection and respect Johnny Kelley inspired.

Above: A Holiday Inn in New London, CT, in August of 1978—the day before Kelley was to run a 12-mile road race nearby.

Right: The Johnny Kelley bobblehead doll.

Johnny Kelley finishes his final Boston Marathon. (Nora Lewis)

Chapter 13
LANDMARK YEARS

"All the hullabaloo really started in '81 because of my fiftieth Boston," Johnny explains. "*Good Morning America* and a bunch of others came down to interview me. Letters started coming in from all over the country, along with all kinds of telephone calls. When I was a young man in my prime, nobody paid this much attention to me."

Since the fitness-crazed general public first learned of Johnny's fiftieth Boston Marathon, his fame has circulated throughout the world. Everyone wants to know, "What makes Johnny run?" He has been featured in hundreds of publications, including *Time* magazine and the *Wall Street Journal*, and television shows ranging from *Real People* to PBS' *Nova*, where he was highlighted in a segment on aging. He holds court regularly in his basement, which doubles as a painting studio and trophy room.

Johnny's easel and painting paraphernalia occupy one corner of his basement. The pervading smell of drying paint and turpentine is overpowering at first, but one's nostrils soon adapt. Finished paintings are mounted just above where he sits and plies his brushes each morning around 8:30. Sunlight spills over his shoulder onto his canvas from large single-paned windows behind him.

The rest of the room is given over to his hundreds of medals, wonderfully ornate trophies, and assorted marathon memorabilia. Though hopelessly tarnished, his very first loving cup is still on dis-

play. His laurel wreath from 1935 hangs on a nearby wall. It is a collection he has been adding to for decades by racing regularly in master and senior competitions. "I'm a serious competitor," Kel stresses.
"I'm not a curiosity. I'm all business." Johnny has donated many of
his awards to road races that benefit worthy causes, otherwise the
room would be completely impassable. A large box of assorted running shoes sits in a corner by the sliding glass door through which
Johnny exits each morning. The pair most recently worn sit by the
threshold and dry in the sun.

"Running is a big, big part of my life," Johnny says, "and so's my
painting. But the most important part is my wife." It was to Laura
that Johnny dedicated his fiftieth Boston Marathon. In a guest col-
umn in the *Boston Herald* on Marathon eve he wrote, "I want to
thank my wife Laura for being so wonderful all these years and putting up with all this stuff. She's helped me in so many ways. For years
she's been super."

The New England Sports Museum honored Johnny's golden
Marathon with a special salute at the John F. Kennedy Library. At
that fete, race director Will Cloney announced that the B.A.A. was
sending John and Laura to Japan. "Each year, the top two American
finishers in the Marathon get a free trip to Japan to run in Ohme,"
Johnny explains. "They always pay for a manager to go too. Jock
Semple went, Will Cloney's gone quite a few times. For my fiftieth,
the B.A.A. sent me and gave us a check to pay Laura's expenses."

Of all the junkets Johnny's been on, the trip to Ohme remains his
favorite. "They love me in Japan." he says. "They have a 10K and a
30K race. I ran the 30K, which is about 18 1/2 miles." In a driving
rain, Johnny ran 2:35:02, which averages out to about a 3:30
marathon. "That was the most wonderful trip of our lives. I'd go back
anytime."

When he arrived at the starting line in Hopkinton, Johnny found
a big green shamrock decorated with the number 50 painted on the
pavement. "Every year since '81 we've had Jacques LeDuc, the man
who paints the starting line, create something for Johnny," says Rob
Phipps, chairman of the Hopkinton Marathon Committee.

Future Olympic gold medalist Joan Benoit Samuelson was running her second Boston Marathon that year, and almost lined up in
Johnny's special spot. "That's how I first found out who he was and

what he means to this race," remembers Samuelson. " 'Don't stand in that space!' they told me. 'Don't stand in that space! That's reserved for Johnny Kelley.' "

"I don't think people realize how special his talents and career have been," says Samuelson. "He's been so competitive for so many years—for *decades!* It's an awesome feat."

A blue and gold banner celebrating Kel's fiftieth was stretched across the finish line when he arrived in 4:01:25, a time that disappointed him. "A lot of the hoopla tired me out. With all the waving to the crowds, my arms got as tired as my legs. I was really beat the last four miles. A lot of runners came up behind me and whacked me on the back to congratulate me. They meant well, but they could've knocked me down. The runners are actually my biggest rooters.

"One year I was running through Framingham, and a girl came running up on my right and said, 'Mr. Kelley, Mr. Kelley! I want to give you a kiss.' I said, 'Well, I'm trying to get to Boston, right now.' She put her hand over her mouth and kissed her hand, then put her hand over my mouth. That's how she kissed me. Took me four miles to get the smile off my face.

"In the Falmouth Road Race last year there was one runner who took a paper cup at every water stop and poured water down my back. I had a bath the whole way!" Johnny laughs.

The first time Johnny Kelley ran the Boston Marathon, distance running was a sport for working-class oddballs. By the time he ran his fiftieth, the nation had marathon mania, and Johnny was the running movement's patriarch. Running shoes had been nonexistent when he began running. Now they were big business, and companies were shipping their latest innovations to his East Dennis retreat by the box load.

But the most revolutionary change of all occurred eight months after his golden Marathon.

In December of '81, the International Amateur Athletic Federation, the world's governing body of track and field, approved the creation of "trust funds," effectively opening the door for athletes to become "professional amateurs." Serious expense and prize money would soon become an accepted part of the running game. Several months earlier, anticipating this milestone decision, B.A.A. president and race director Will Cloney had sought and received authorization from the club's Board of Governors to pursue commercial sponsorship and to execute such agreements as he saw fit.

Will Cloney's association with the grand old Marathon went back to the '30s. For years he had emphatically insisted that the event remain purely the domain of amateurs. But realizing these radical new changes could ruin the race he had nurtured through its rapid, difficult growth, he began to waver. Big money marathons in New York, Chicago, and London were poised to lure the world's best away from Boston. Cloney was still skeptical of the new rules, but he wanted to be ready. At the very least, commercial sponsorship was badly needed to administer the Marathon properly. Office space and a full-time staff were necessary. Such a world-renowned event could no longer be orchestrated out of Jock Semple's Salon de Rubdown.

While the size and shape of distance running continued to evolve, Johnny Kelley was relishing his new-found role as a spokesman for his sport. He and Laura began attending races and clinics throughout the country, where charmed audiences listen to Johnny's anecdotes and advice. "I tell them about Mr. K's three Ds," Johnny explains. "Desire, Determination, and Dedication. 'You don't have to run a marathon to be in shape,' I tell them. The heck with the marathon. It's important not to be a couch potato. We don't wear out, we rest out. Do something. Walking, biking, whatever. I do some swimming myself." Johnny has done his "missionary" work everywhere, from Seattle to Cleveland, from Florida to Texas. "Of course I have to sing 'em a little song," he chuckles.

"Young at Heart" is Johnny Kelley's anthem. He'll sing it a cappella at the drop of a hat. At home, he might surprise a guest by switching on a tape player and doing a duet with Ol' Blue Eyes himself. "I'm a professional artist and an amateur singer," Johnny says, before launching into song.

After his February trip to Ohme, Johnny continued to prepare for his 51st Boston and his 100th marathon overall. He has maintained the same training formula for decades. "I start to get ready after Christmas by adding a long workout of 2 hours every other week or so. I always take a day off after the long run."

But while Johnny prepared for yet another 26-mile trot from Hopkinton to Boston, the future of the Marathon was becoming wrapped in controversy. In February of '82, the *Boston Globe* reported that Will Cloney had signed a contract with one Marshall Medoff, authorizing this little-known Boston attorney to act as exclusive agent for the Marathon and solicit sponsors. This Medoff had done, signing up several corporate giants. The press portrayed Cloney's actions as clandestine, and the financial arrangement with Medoff, the outsider, as far too open-ended. Medoff could keep any funds he raised above a certain amount. Cloney had seriously underestimated how much money could be raised. Medoff had done a phenomenal job, and was said to be pocketing more money than the race itself. Cloney vigorously denied all accusations, but public debate and angry criticism were rampant.

Two weeks before the race, the Prudential Insurance Company, upset by the disclosure that commercial sponsors were being recruited, decided to end its support of the Marathon, effective in '83. The race could still finish in front of the "Pru" on Ring Road, but the free use of facilities and the underwriting of more than $100,000 in expenses were withdrawn. The '82 race, a thrilling duel between Alberto Salazar and Dick Beardsley, seemed little more than a momentary break in the hostilities. On June 16th, an embattled Will Cloney resigned after 36 years as volunteer director of the Boston Marathon, citing health reasons. A former newspaperman himself, Cloney said he was ashamed of the way the media had handled the story. In September, the B.A.A. filed suit against Medoff, seeking to declare his contract invalid.

"I've always been a Cloney fan," Johnny says. "I felt very sorry for Will. He admitted to me that he made a big mistake. Everybody makes mistakes. We're still good friends. He has a race up in Scituate every year and I go and fire the starting gun, y' know, do some public relations work. Will has always been a perfect gentleman. He would never have done anything intentional to damage the race. He loved the Boston Marathon."

The summer after Johnny ran his 52nd B.A.A., he was honored by the President's Council on Physical Fitness and Sports for being the person over 60 who had devoted most of his life to fitness. Because of this honor, Johnny was invited to go to Dallas, where his fitness would be put to the test at Dr. Kenneth Cooper's well known Aerobics Center. On his first ever treadmill test, Johnny placed in the superior category for men 27 years his junior. "Well if that's so,"

Johnny said, smiling, "why the hell can't I win races anymore?"

At age 76 he had a treadmill time of 24 minutes, and a perfect EKG reading. At the time, former Cowboys quarterback Roger Staubach, a man half Johnny's age, held the treadmill record of 30 minutes. Johnny insisted that if he hadn't been weary from two previous days of exhaustive testing, he could've broken Staubach's record. While at the Center, Johnny ran the last thirteen miles of the White Rock Marathon in Dallas and established an unofficial age-group record by nearly 22 minutes, averaging 7:52 per mile.

"We've gone every year since," Johnny says. "They always plan my trip in conjunction with the White Rock Marathon and I run the last half of the race—not the whole thing. Boston's the only marathon for me. Last year they said my bone scan was remarkable. I made another record on the treadmill and all that stuff. They give me a complete overall checkup."

"Johnny has phenomenal cardiovascular fitness," says aerobics guru Dr. Cooper. "At 84, his level of conditioning is equal to that of a man in his late 50s, early 60s. He's quite a specimen."

Through the mid '80s, the requests for Johnny to speak at races and receptions continued to multiply. The number of people trying to contact Johnny by phone actually became trying for several other gentlemen named John Kelley who also make their home on Cape Cod. "The other John Kelleys were getting my calls, and it started to annoy them. They were getting dragged out of the shower and stuff like that."

To curtail the problem, Johnny and the telephone company got together. Mr. Boston Marathon is now listed in the Cape Cod phone book as: 'KELLEY JOHN A. (MARATHON).' "Sometimes I get calls for the other John Kelleys. One of them is a doctor, and people call and want me to prescribe medication. They call me 'Doctor Kelley.' They call me a lot of other things too!"

The Test of Time
by James F. Fixx

John A. Kelley has been a runner for 62 years. New research shows he has the physical condition of a fit 40-year-old. What does this mean for the rest of us?

Is age no longer sacred? Here we are at Dr. Kenneth H. Cooper's Aerobics Center in Dallas, and John Adelbert Kelley, 76 years old and soon to run his 53rd Boston Marathon, is gasping and laboring while a treadmill of forbidding incline grinds away underneath his bright blue running flats. He is puffing noisily, sweat flowing along taut cheekbones. Wires dangle from his bare chest, and a rhythmic electronic tone offers amplified confirmation that his heart is not merely beating in the customary manner but is very nearly giving its all.

One would think that any person witnessing Kelley's ordeal would, with alarm, start hunting for the "Off" switch. But Cooper, the author of *Aerobics*, *The New Aerobics* and an apparently unending series of best-selling sequels, is not, at this moment anyway, in a compassionate frame of mind. After all, he has got Kelley on that treadmill for a reason; to garner further evidence that a lifetime of exercise improves health and enhances longevity. "You've still got a lot left," he insists, studying a digital clock's angular red numerals. "Keep it up." His subject, though clearly unconvinced, stalwartly pushes on.

How Kelley, a retired maintenance worker for the Boston Edison Company, came to find himself in this hard-breathing predicament is a tale that begins 62 years ago this spring in Boston. At 15, he arrived home from baseball practice one afternoon to learn that the legendary Clarence H. DeMar ("Mr. DeMarathon") had won the annual Patriots' Day Marathon for the second time. Something about the notion of trying to run 26 or so miles appealed to the bandy-legged youngster's sense of the impossible, or at least the improbable. Soon afterward, he quit his left fielder's post ("I couldn't hit very well anyway") and volunteered his services to the Medford High School track team.

The decision was a historic one. Johnny, as he is universally known, has gone running on all but a few of the 22,600-odd days since then. He has competed in 111 marathons (2:28:18 PR set in 1940) and won twelve of them (including Boston twice), been a member of three Olympic teams (1936, 1940, and 1948), and competed in no fewer than 1,500 foot-races.

Although his astonishingly unwrinkled, hawk-like face is now seen farther back in the field than in his heyday, he still posts thoroughly respectable times. Last June, near his home on Cape Cod, he ran a ten-kilometer race in "forty-two or forty-three" minutes, and in December he set an unofficial world half-marathon record for men his age (1:42:50) during the White Rock Marathon in Dallas. On a good day, he can run a marathon in under four hours.

But Johnny Kelley is not just an outstanding athlete—he's also a medical godsend. Although researchers are fairly confident that long-term exercise can promote better health and even a longer life, the current running boom is still so young that there are almost no examples of people who have spent 50 or more years engaged in daily aerobic activity. In the natural order of things, athletes tend sooner or later to suffer injuries that curtail their participation, or they simply grow weary of the rigors of sustained training. Neither, however, has happened to Johnny, whose racing times held fairly steady until he was nearly 60 years old and who trains with gusto even today. Kelley is therefore a rare piece in the overall puzzle. For decades, researchers have expressed considerable interest in trying to determine what has kept him running and, even more importantly, what influence his unremitting exercise regimen has had on him.

Early one morning last summer, while in Boston to accept an award from the President's Council on Physical Fitness and Sports, Johnny went out for a run. By chance he encountered fellow runner Dr. Ken Cooper. As they ran together through the streets, Cooper popped the familiar question. "I'd sure like to get you down to the Aerobics Center and see what makes you tick," he said.

Because Johnny had known Cooper since the 1950s (and had in fact coached him in his first marathon efforts), and also because by this time Johnny had developed his own curiosity about how he managed to continue doing what he does, he agreed to pay a visit. Cooper and Kelley decided upon a three-day period in early December, and soon afterward invited me to join them in order to chronicle what would prove a significant investigation, filled with implications for all of us as we age and as we run.

In the decades since his prime, Kelley's running pace has slowed, but his ability to attract awards and honors has not. He was recently inducted into the National Track and Field Hall of Fame. He is an honorary colonel in the Massachusetts State Police. (Walter Cronkite is also a member, but as a colonel Johnny outranks him.) And the New England Telephone Company, which is not celebrated for its whimsy, has granted him a special listing in the Cape Cod directory: "Kelley John A. (Marathon)."

All this might suggest that Johnny has become more celebrity than athlete. Not at all. He works out for an hour or more seven days a week, averaging a total of 60 to 65 miles. He does hill work and speed work (repeat 300s and all-out half-mile efforts) twice a week and increases his runs to two-and-one-half hours in preparation for an important event. "When I run a race," he says, "I'm out for blood. I want to do my best.

I never start in the middle of the pack. I position myself toward the front, either on the left or the right. That way I get a good fast start."

Last Thanksgiving morning Johnny competed in a 10-km race in Clearwater, Florida. Because it was 80 degrees and humid, his time of 47:02 was not particularly satisfying. All the same, he finished in the top third of the field. "I've still got the stuff," he told a friend afterwards.

The question in Ken Cooper's mind, however, as he awaited Johnny's visit was: How *much* stuff? The various measures of physical ability characteristically decline with age. Strength, speed, endurance and reaction time all wane as the heart's maximum rate slows, muscle girth diminishes and nerves respond more sluggishly. It was probable, said Cooper before the examination, that in Johnny's case these changes had occurred less markedly than in the typical 76 year old, but he had no way of guessing how much less.

At the Aerobics Center, a campus-like complex through which a mile-long running path meanders, a computer contains detailed records of some 30,000 men and women who have been studied there since 1970. Therefore, once Johnny had been evaluated, it would be possible to assign him his proper physiological age. This, Cooper explained, is a far more accurate index of overall health than chronological age.

Johnny had visited only four doctors in his lifetime and did not relish the thought of breaking tradition on this occasion, "I don't even *have* a doctor of my own," he said. "You never know what those guys are going to find." With his wife Laura along for moral support, Johnny checked into the Aerobics Center's guest lodge and after a restless night's sleep reported to Cooper early the next day.

The institute is equipped with state-of-the-art medical instrumentation that, in the minds of clients, more than justifies the $820 fee levied for the most comprehensive examination. Wearing a blue warm-up suit presented by Japanese admirers, Johnny filled out a medical history. His replies were those of a healthy young man. He had had a tonsillectomy as a child and a hernia operation 15 years ago, otherwise there was nothing to report. "I've had no illnesses and only one injury in 55 years," he said.

The injury, he explained, occurred not as a result of running but because of Laura's suggesting that they take up square dancing. "She got a sore hip and I twisted my knee," said Johnny. "That was enough of square dancing."

Johnny's evaluation began with the usual measurements: height (5'6"), weight (131 pounds), waist girth (31 inches), blood pressure (110/78), resting heart rate (52). As the tests continued over the three days, Cooper said, Johnny would progress through 24 stations until, on the last day, he would undergo the most demanding procedure of all, the treadmill endurance test, which has pushed more than one top athlete, including all-pro quarterback Roger Staubach and champion tennis player Ken Rosewall, to their outermost, gasping limits.

In a laboratory, exercise physiologist Jill Upton, who has herself competed in five marathons, checked Johnny's VO_2 max, or oxygen-processing capacity. Because the ability to use oxygen governs the rate at which muscles can do their work, physiologists regard VO_2 max as perhaps the single most reliable indicator of an individual's condition. Johnny's was 46.48— "superior even for a 50 year old in good shape," commented Upton. "This is most definitely unusual for a man his age."

Studying Kelley's EKG, Upton remarked with surprise that she could detect none of the irregularities common in the elderly. "This is the cardiogram of an athlete," she said. "His heart could belong to a 16-year-old."

Upton's observation may have been more accurate
than she realized. At noon Johnny, Laura and I walked
over to the Aerobics Center cafeteria for a sandwich.
Passing a pretty young staff member whom Johnny
had met earlier, he rolled his eyes like Groucho Marx,
wheeled around, and started off in mock pursuit.

After lunch a Polaroid photograph was taken of
Johnny in his running shorts. "Jeepers creepers!" he
exclaimed, "I look as if I don't have any legs." (His legs
do seem somewhat short in proportion to his torso, a
fact that may confer a biomechanical advantage since
he needs to move less limb mass in running than would
otherwise be the case.) His lung capacity was tested
and proven to be seven percent higher than normal for
a man his age. His eyesight checked out at 20/20. And,
although he has never done weight training, he was
able to press 185 pounds of Universal chrome with his
arms and 190 with his legs.

"Good job!" exclaimed the lab technician after he
had accomplished this.

"Holy Toledo!" said Johnny. "Can you imagine what
I could do if I ever decided to practice?"

Over the next two days Kelley underwent a variety of
tests. Other than an elevated glucose level ("only slightly above what would be considered normal for a man 76
years of age . . . [but which may indicate] early onset
diabetes," said Cooper) and some hearing loss, he was in
perfect health. His vision and reflexes were excellent,
his blood pressure low. Lab tests showed normal
amounts of potassium, chloride, calcium, sodium, phos-
phorus, protein and other substances. It was a remarkable showing for a man his age. As the tests continued,
word of the results began to spread among Cooper's
staff. At one point Dr. Arnie Jensen, a radiologist,
stopped by and, looking Johnny over, said wryly, "I wish
this guy would do something about getting in shape."

But the treadmill test loomed ahead. The treadmill is
installed in a small room in Cooper's own suite of

offices. Its belt moves at a constant speed but its slope increases each minute, insuring that even the best-conditioned athlete will ultimately cry uncle. If Johnny could last more than 21 minutes, Cooper said, it would be a remarkable performance for a man his age.

Technician Harold Buckhalter fastened a blood pressure cuff to Johnny's left arm and wired him to an EKG in order to monitor vital functions. As preparations continued, onlookers began to gather: Dr. R.L. Bohannon, former Surgeon General of the Air Force and currently one of Cooper's medical consultants; Roy Busby, a North Texas State University journalism professor who serves as publicity advisor to the Aerobics Center; a photographer assigned to record the historic proceedings; several others.

Cooper flipped a switch and the treadmill started rolling. Johnny moved along easily, his heart rate barely elevated above resting level. Cooper glanced at the instruments. "That EKG is absolutely perfect," he said. "I'll swap hearts with you any day, Johnny—no questions asked."

Several minutes passed; Johnny showed no signs of effort. Cooper glanced at the dock. "You've reached the 'good' category for women over 60," he said. Johnny made a wry face. His heart rate was 129. Amplified electronically, its thump filled the room.

Studying Johnny's face, Cooper asked how he was feeling. Although working harder now, Johnny gave a thumbs-up. "You're looking great," said Cooper.

The clock read 18:30. Johnny, sweating heavily, was concentrating. "Everything looks good," said Cooper. "We're coming up on 20 minutes."

Suddenly the treadmill emitted an unfamiliar creak. Cooper, clearly concerned, said "Try to stay toward the front, Johnny. Don't let yourself fall off." Johnny, by this time climbing a formidable incline, was puffing. His heart rate was 161, nearly 20 beats per minute faster than the average 76 year old is capable of.

Consulting a chart, Cooper said, "You've just passed the 'superior' category for 50-year-old men," he said. "You can say goodbye to those guys."

Johnny did not respond. Cooper looked worried. "Is that enough for you?" he asked. Johnny shook his head and once again displayed a winner's thumbs-up. His heartbeat, though trip-hammer-fast, was as regular as a metronome.

Cooper, pleased, said, "You just made 'superior' for 40-year-old men, and you're not far from 'superior' for 30-year-old men."

Finally, when the clock read 24 minutes, Johnny gasped, "That's about it." The treadmill slowed and he walked for a while, cooling down and catching his breath. "An outstanding performance!" said Cooper.

When he was able to talk, Johnny asked, "How long did Staubach last on this thing?"

Thirty minutes, he was told. Johnny looked disappointed. "I was after his record," he said.

Later that day Cooper reviewed for me what he felt he had learned from the examination. Johnny's physical condition, he said, is comparable to that of the top four percent of men 40 to 49 years old. He has lost some hearing but is otherwise in excellent shape. "We're looking at a man 25 to 30 years younger than his chronological age," Cooper told me. "Even allowing for good genes, it's my guess that it's exercise that has kept him young.

"I'm convinced," said Cooper, "that the gerontology textbooks are perpetuating a myth. Most of the decline that comes with age isn't inevitable at all. It's caused by disuse. We're still a long way from knowing the limits of human capacities."

Among other results, Johnny's performance buttresses the findings of the celebrated Framingham heart disease study, which suggests that exercise is not just a desirable but an essential component of a healthy life. "Kelley's condition doesn't surprise me at all," observes Dr. Charles Steinmetz, a preventive medicine specialist and a close follower of the Framingham findings. "It's generally recognized that the human life span can be greatly increased. There's no reason why we shouldn't be active to the age of 100. Rather than try to sort out all the fad diets that come our way, chances are all we need is a modest exercise program to help us live the kind of life Johnny Kelley is still enjoying."

While Cooper and I had been talking it had begun to rain—a gray, sodden drizzle. Hurrying back to my room at the guest lodge, I saw Johnny for the second time that day. He was out running, alone, splashing through the cold puddles. He looked utterly content.

The late James F. Fixx was the author of *The Complete Book of Running*, several other best-selling books and numerous articles on running.

Chapter 14
NEW DAYS, NEW HEROES

$\mathscr{T}$he 1985 Boston Marathon was the fiftieth anniversary of Johnny Kelley's first victory. The fabled event was still mired in lawsuits and criticism stemming from the Marshall Medoff affair. The B.A.A.'s Board of Governors was spending in excess of $500,000 on lawyers, but almost nothing on runners. Meanwhile, the New York and Chicago Marathons were attracting all the elite athletes with prize and appearance money. Upstart races in Pittsburgh and New Jersey were also assembling fields superior to the world's oldest annual marathon by offering hefty purses. Tradition alone was no longer enough of a lure.

After staging two consecutive non-events, the B.A.A. offered a meager concession in '85. It announced that it would pay hotel expenses for some of the top runners. But in '85 there was only one elite runner in the field. Geoff Smith of England, easy race winner in '84, ran Boston sporting the logo of Prime Computer on his chest. The Natick-based company had paid him to do so. Fighting severe heat and muscle cramps, Smith walked several times and still won by more than five minutes, in 2:14:05. "If I'd have been in a competition, I could have run 2:10," Smith told Joe Concannon of the *Globe*.

There was little fanfare or excitement at the front of the race, but rambling along far back in the pack, Johnny Kelley, king of the Marathon, did not disappoint his loyal subjects. Despite being

plagued by stomach problems most of the way, he stayed the course
for the 51st time in 54 attempts, in 4:31. "I had to walk a bit on the
hills," Johnny conceded, "but the crowds got me through it again. I
don't know many of their names, but year after year I see the same
faces. They always wait for me and I just try to not keep them waiting too long."

Two months after his 78th birthday, Johnny received yet another
prize honoring his inspiring achievements. At a ceremony held at the
United Nations, Johnny was presented with the Abebe Bikila Award
by New York Marathon director Fred LeBow. (Bikila was the great
Ethiopian runner who won both the '60 and '64 Olympic marathons
but was left paralyzed after an auto accident.) The honor is given
annually for outstanding contributions to long distance running.
Other recipients include Emil Zatopek, Frank Shorter, Crete Waitz
and Bikila's countryman, Mamo Wolde.

"I met Bikila in '63 when he came over with Wolde to run
Boston. They came over five or six weeks early to train on the course
and stayed in Lexington with Dr. Warren Guild, a friend of mine. I
played ping pong with Bikila. Every time I'd stoop over to pick up
the ball, I'd turn around and he'd be doing calisthenics. You can't
deny his record. He was one of the finest in the world."

As the Boston Marathon's 90th birthday approached, the once-
proud pageant was badly showing its age. No longer the world's pre-
mier endurance test, the race was clearly on the brink. Meanwhile,
the courts ruled that Marshall Medoff's contract with the B.A.A. was
null and void. A revamped Board of Governors, seeking to restore the
race to its proper international status, began seeking the commercial
sponsorship it sorely needed. On September 4th, the B.A.A. consum-
mated a 10-year, $10-million deal with John Hancock Mutual Life
Insurance. (This arrangement was replaced by a 15-year, $18-million
deal in '89.) Hancock would now put up all the prize money
($250,000 in '86), and cover all the finish line costs. It was agreed that
the start of the race would remain in Hopkinton, but the finish would
be moved further down Boylston Street near the entrance to the
Boston Public Library and in the shadow of the John Hancock Tower.

Boston's first run for funds immediately brought the world's elite
back to town. Australia's Rob deCastella was the day's biggest winner.
Along with a Mercedes-Benz and $30,000 for winning, deCastella

pocketed $25,000 for his new course record (2:07:51), and $5,000 for running a sub-2:10. Hancock also gave the mustachioed Aussie a one-year, $75,000 personal services contract that was reportedly doubled after his victory. Ingrid Kristiansen, the women's winner, took home $35,000 for her triumph. "I never won a dime," Johnny says. "New days, new heroes, new gods. I think Hancock brought the race back to where it should be. I felt sorry for the Prudential people, but the Boston Marathon is back to being the greatest in the world right now."

Each year, John Hancock also gives the B.A.A. a lump sum, which is distributed to the eight cities and towns through which the Marathon passes, in appreciation for their ongoing support of the race.

Another of Hancock's commitments to the Marathon was the creation of Running and Fitness Clinics. Instead of paying outright appearance money to elite runners, Hancock hires these world-class performers to conduct the extremely popular clinics in area schools. Johnny is a charter member of this program, which includes Bill Rodgers, Joan Benoit Samuelson, Ibrahim Hussein and many other international competitors.

"At first the kids are skeptical when they see Johnny at the clinics," says Jack Mahoney of Hancock. " 'What can a man in his 80s teach me about running?,' they seem to be thinking. But Johnny is a natural entertainer. He captivates them with his talk. Then he takes them out on a track or in the gym and keeps up with them. He really wins them over. He wins *everybody* over."

For the past three years, John Hancock has provided Johnny with a few other much deserved perks. "Hancock pays all our expenses now. They provide a limousine that takes us up to Boston, and they put us up at the Copley Plaza. DeMar used to say 'The older you get, the better they treat you.' I guess he was right!"

For many years after their move to Cape Cod, Johnny and Laura spent the night before the Marathon with an old friend in Belmont. "One year I was up in Framingham training with the state troopers, and I decided to make a reservation at a motel in Milford so we'd be closer to Hopkinton. But that was dullsville! Then for three years we stayed right in Hopkinton with the family of Paul Phipps, who's a member of the B.A.A. Board of Governors."

Johnny Kelley is now an honorary citizen of Hopkinton. ("That
means I don't have to pay taxes.") During the years the Kelleys
stayed there, the town's Marathon Committee always took them out
for dinner so Johnny could have his last big pre-race meal. "I have
my steak the night before now, not the morning of the race. I can't
do that anymore. In the morning, I have scrambled eggs, half a
grapefruit, some toast and coffee. I can't be bothered with that carbo
loading stuff. I'm too old to worry about all that."

One thing Johnny does worry about is milk. He hates it. "When I
was in kindergarten at the Mead Street School in Charlestown, the
teacher—I can see her now—she came down with a bottle of milk
and a straw while I was working on a clay model, and said, 'This'll
make you a big strong boy.' I was so sick from it.

"I put hot water on my cereal. I've done it since I was five years
old. I take calcium pills now as a supplement. I like ice cream and
custard, but a plain glass of milk—I can't even look at it."

During the years Johnny and Laura spent Marathon eve in
Hopkinton, the Phipps were busy shielding Johnny, keeping the
wolves away from the door. But in truth, Johnny likes to do a bit of
howling himself. "Everyone in Hopkinton was very nice to us, but
there were no parties, no jive. In Boston, now, we're where the
action is."

"He'd rather the partying was after the race than before," says
Laura.

"In the old days," Johnny says, "we'd run the race and all the fun
and games were held after. Last year, there was a little too much of
it—press conferences, receptions. I thought Monday morning would
never come. The only thing that kind of bothers me is when people
come up to me for an autograph while I'm having dinner. Laura tells
them to wait 'til after. She's my agent. I don't understand these athletes today who charge $10 for an autograph. They annoy me. I don't
go along with that."

❖

Ol' John Could Have Earned Megabucks

At today's prices, Kelley's 54 Boston Marathon runs would have been worth $288,200 in prize money; however, at age 78, Monday's 55th trip down Memory Lane will be priceless for the Gingerbread Boy

April 16, 1986
by JERRY NASON
Special to the *Globe*

John Adelbert Kelley, formerly of Arlington and Acton, now of East Dennis, plans to perambulate in the Boston Athletic Association–John Hancock Megabucks Marathon Monday.

It will be Boston race No. 55 for him, the first with purse money on the line.

At age 78, Kelley doesn't expect to win a dime.

However, I appear amid the congregation today to announce that—retroactively and by my careful accounting—the sponsors of this suddenly purse-monied Marathon are probably owin' Kel $288,200.

In deferred payments, so to speak, for his past deeds performed in and with utter devotion to this hoary event.

When informed via phone of the result of this financial analysis of the 20 times he has finished within what are now pay-off positions, Kelley positively cackled with glee.

"$288,200? Wow! I'll take it!" he whooped.

This projection is not performed entirely in jest. Kelley, after all, is the treasured last active link between the Marathon's good ol' days of beef stew and laurel wreath handouts and the march to the mint race that begins this year. What fragments now remain of the great race traditions of the past—well, Kelley is the glue, baby! Believe it.

Although Kel's past Boston victories numbered

merely two (at $30,000 per pop at the '86 wage scale), his astonishing total of *seven* second places would, alone, have prospered him to the cash-register tune of $140,000.

In addition to which he has finished third, twice fourth, thrice fifth, and so on and so on, up to $288,200 (see accompanying chart).

"I *knew* I was born too soon," groaned Kelley.

Well, at the very least, the money baggers of the B.A.A.–John Hancock combine will dispatch a chauffeured limousine to pick you up at East Dennis on game day and get you to Hopkinton on time?

"There you go, kidding again," chortled John. "No. Laura and I are planning on driving up Saturday, two days before the race, and have lunch somewhere along the way. Then we will be staying with friends in Hopkinton until Tuesday.

"But I have been riding limousine-style lately. Have been doing some running clinics for Hancock, and they provide a limousine for me. Judd Perry, from over in Bourne, drove me to Ashland, Wellesley and Boston College High. These clinics are supposed to keep the towns along the course happy."

And with no possible purse money dangling like a carrot ahead of him in the big race, how much "happiness" does John A. Kelley anticipate on the occasion of his 55th long journey afoot down the 26 miles from Hopkinton?

He, whose personal reference to himself is The Gingerbread Boy, ("Catch me if you can!") pondered for a moment, then remarked:

"Well, it's become a pretty emotional thing for me . . . a sort of 'Old Home Week' celebration. So many familiar faces along the way, hundreds of them. Some of those faces, here and there, I'm able to put names on, but mostly it's a run down Memory Lane for me, with all those faces smiling and urging me on."

Ol' John doesn't have to agitate about such things as

tactics, strategy and opponents anymore. He was a notorious worrywart back in the old days, probably fretted and sweated himself out of two or three more victories.

Water over the dam. Kel's 55th is what now matters.

He said, "I will run, but sort of look things over carefully at first, see what kind of a day it is out there.

"At this point in my life, I'm not going to risk injury or endanger my health. If the ol' body protests too much, you can count on me to bum a ride the rest of the way—even if I'll be heartbroken not to say 'Hello' to some of those wonderful roadside fans who wait for me farther down the course. I look forward to seeing them every year.

"Even without your $288,200, hah, I have much to be thankful for. I'm still alive, for starters. I have a wonderful wife, a comfortable home and nice friends. I'm grateful for them all.

"By the way, how much interest has accrued on that $288,200 of yours?"

Exit Kelley, laughing!

Johnny Kelley's "Non-earnings"

Place	1986 Value	Kelley finishes	Purse Value
First	$30,000	1935, 1945	$60,000
Second	$20,000	'34, '37, '40, '41, '43, '44, '46	$140,000
Third	$15,000	1938	$15,000
Fourth	$12,000	1948, 1949	$24,000
Fifth	$10,000	'36, '42, '50	$30,000
Sixth	$8,500	1951	$8,500
Seventh	$7,000	1953	$7,000
Twelfth	$1,300	1952	$1,300
Thirteenth	$1,200	1939, 1947	$2,400
Total:			$288,200

Source: Jerry Nason

Bill Rodgers on Johnny Kelley: An Interview by Richard A. Johnson

To sit informally in the back room of the Bill Rodgers Running Center in Boston's fashionable Quincy Market and observe the store's namesake expounding with characteristic enthusiasm about Johnny Kelley, is to witness first-hand the runner who has been called the sport's "Peter Pan." Displaying a studious yet animated demeanor perfectly suited to his former occupation as a teacher, the former four-time Boston Marathon champion is eager to discuss both his personal experiences with Kelley and the lasting significance of Johnny's never-ending running career. Rodgers, now forty-three, is currently devoting much of his time to his family and sporting goods business, while exploring new horizons as an elite masters runner.

Sixteen years after his first Boston triumph, Rodgers is still considered one of the primary spokespeople for the new breed of professional runner. He is one of the few members of this fraternity who competed both within the strictures of the now anachronistic "amateur" system—which also bound Kelley—as well as the new open professionial system.

His reflections on the runner he still refers to as "John the Elder" were shared in his miniature museum of an office while customers and employees scurried around us.

Q. *When did you first learn of Johnny Kelley and when did you first meet?*
A. Well, when I first ran the Boston Marathon in 1973 I know that I must have heard of him. However, it didn't really sink in until 1975, when I won the race. Shortly thereafter I was invited to run in a charity Mother's Day road race in Newton . . . Well, as it turned

out, Johnny was also invited and I finally got to meet him. He came up to me and we hit it off right away. He was his usual ebullient, excited self while congratulating me on my Boston win. We've been friends ever since, and with time, I've come to learn of Johnny's records and accomplishments.

Q. *When you were in high school was he someone you recognized as a running hero?*

A. In high school I ran only one road race and that was the Manchester Thanksgiving Day race, where I won the high school division. At the time I only knew one road runner and that was Amby Burfoot, who would later be my cross-country and track teammate at Wesleyan University. I had also heard of local collegiate stars such as Art Dulong, John Vitale and Ray Carruthers.

Later on I would race against Pat McMahon while I was at Wesleyan, but I really wasn't a road runner . . . at the time I had no interest in the roads. Not only was I unaware of Johnny Kelley in high school but, growing up in Hartford, Connecticut I didn't even know about the Boston Marathon! We had our own very intense high school track and cross-country rivalries to occupy us.

Q. *Can you share some personal anecdotes about Johnny?*

A. I can think of one particularly humorous incident which took place while Johnny and I were conducting a John Hancock Running Clinic. It seems as though we were at some runners' expo with crowds gathered 'round us, and one runner asked me how many years I had been running. Without thinking I said twenty-five or -six years, forgetting that Johnny was right beside me. Before I knew it, Johnny smiled and replied that he had been running for over sixty years. It just floored me at the time and only then really began to sink in. It still floors me!

I like what he has always said about running being

a labor of love. It truly is a labor and you have to love it to really push at it and excel.

I have a painting by Johnny in my office of some deer running over sand dunes on a beach, and that painting means a lot to me because it was presented to me by the Special Olympics in honor of the Jingle Bells Benefit Race—and because it's by Johnny. Apparently he had donated the painting to them knowing I would receive it.

When I think of Johnny I think not only of him, but of his wife Laura, who is super friendly. I also think of his career, when he was working for all those years and how he lived in a completely different era of sports. I compare it to today, where amateurs have since become professionals.

More than any one incident, or even the sixty Boston Marathons, the one thing I always think about in regard to Johnny is his personality.

Just contemplating running sixty Boston Marathons is impossible—it's like counting to a million. I also recognize and respect Johnny for his Olympic teams and victories, but his spirit is what keeps shining through. After all, that's what enables him to continue his amazing career.

Q. *Did you think of Johnny when you won your first Boston Marathon, and was it apparent to you that you'd joined a very exclusive club with members such as DeMar, Pawson, Burfoot, et al.?*

A. When I first won Boston I was more shocked than anything. I do remember thinking that this was something I could share with Amby Burfoot because we were so close and because it hadn't been that long since he won the race. However later on I did think about it, and felt that each year I just had to win another—much in the same manner that Johnny went about preparing for the race.

In fact, I sense that Johnny felt even more this way than myself and still does. After all he's reached sixty and we're still counting. Put simply, no one loves the Boston Marathon more than Johnny Kelley. Who could possibly love the Boston Marathon more than Johnny Kelley? (Rodgers breaks out laughing.)

I think that because Johnny is from the Boston area the race must have had a tremendous impact on him from an early age. None of the other marathon greats to my knowledge grew up in metropolitan Boston, certainly not DeMar, Cote, Pawson, Amby, Johnny the Younger, etc. . . . Johnny has a great sense of history and his place within it.

Q. *Do you aspire to emulate Johnny in terms of running the Boston Marathon for years to come? After all, it has been a tradition for former champs such as DeMar and the two Kelleys to continue.*

A. I don't think I will, because I can't possibly envision it. While I certainly want to keep fit, my only remaining goal is to try to set the American Masters record for the marathon. In fact I've been training for this for the past 3½ years and would like nothing better than to set the record at Boston. If I could do that, then I'd feel as though my marathon career was complete. At that point, I'd probably retire from running marathons and continue to compete in shorter races.

The training for marathons is too difficult and competes with other aspects of my life. Starting this year, I'm only training for one marathon per year. In the past I've always run a lot more. Who knows how much longer I'll run them . . . probably not much longer . . . (pause) I can always be a fan! (laughter)

Q. *What do you think Johnny's legacy will be?*

A. To me he's an international sports figure. He is also the spokesperson for the Boston Marathon. That's his ultimate identity. He's known best right here in Boston. His record is what he'll always be known for. For example DeMar is known for his seven wins, an achievement I seriously doubt will ever be challenged. Likewise, Johnny has established the standard for consistency and longevity. This will be his legacy as well as the memories of his attitude, personality, and heart.

Q. *Do you agree with the case that's been made on behalf of Johnny that he should be recognized as perhaps the most remarkable American male athlete of the 20th century?*

A. He is certainly one of the most remarkable, without a doubt. I don't think he's received the national recognition he deserves. He does at Boston Marathon time, especially when it dawns on people that he is twice as old as George Foreman. It also shocks people to learn that at age 84 he can run twenty-six miles. Why, not long ago the country was swooning over Jimmy Connors, and he's only thirty-nine!

You can look at excellence from different angles and Johnny's angle is that he is truly a great endurance athlete. Back when Johnny was an elite athlete, the public and much of the press didn't understand our sport. To Johnny's everlasting credit he has endured long enough to endear himself to the present era, where his accomplishments, both past and present, are celebrated for their true significance.

Bill Rodgers was twenty-seven years old when he won his first Boston Marathon in 1975—the same age as Johnny Kelley when the latter won his first Boston in 1935. Both men continued to draw the lion's share of applause on their annual Patriot's Day run.

Chapter 15
"I'M GONNA MAKE IT!"

$\mathcal{I}$n 1987 and '88, Johnny was still running Boston in less than 4 hours and 30 minutes. It wasn't until '89, at age 81, that he slowed to 5:05, which was his time again in 1990. "My running in the Marathon now is a fast walk. That's really what it is, just my own diddley-daddley pace. But if I'm in a 10K, that's different. I *run*."

Incredibly, in the Fall of 1990, Johnny found himself training for his *sixtieth* Boston Marathon. "If someone had told me back in 1928 that I'd be running sixty Bostons, I would've told them they were nuts."

All told, Johnny has run 118 marathons and more than 1,500 races. In honor of the man and his marathons, the Greater Boston Jimmy Fund, which raises money for research and treatment of children with cancer, chose Johnny as their New England Sports Hero of the Year. Previous honorees include Ted Williams, Bobby Orr and Marvin Hagler. "Six hundred people came, and we raised money for the Jimmy Fund," Johnny says. "I had all five of my sisters with me. They invited other former winners of the Marathon, and we had runners who had won it sixteen times, counting my two wins. Bill Rodgers, Greg Meyer and all that crowd. I sang 'It's A Lovely Way To Spend An Evening.' It was the greatest night of my life. I even got a kiss from Joanie Benoit."

The fact that the evening raised money to help children with cancer pleased Johnny as much as his being the guest of honor. Johnny's favorite charity is the Cape Cod Hospital. Every Memorial Day weekend, a local radio station puts on the Johnny Kelley Half Marathon. Proceeds benefit the hospital. "We get about 800 runners every year, and we've raised almost $40,000 dollars so far," Johnny says proudly.

In April of '91 the news media once again converged on Cedar Hill. "All the local stations came. NBC spent three hours filming me. They had me running around the block and everything, and they put about 45 seconds on the tube," Johnny says, shaking his head. "I got mail from all over the country, plus I did a bunch of telephone interviews. By the time the race came along I was pretty well tired out."

On Marathon morning, good friend State Police Sgt. Dan Donovan picked Johnny and Laura up at the Copley and drove them to Hopkinton, where they would meet up with Johnny's running escorts. "Before the race in '90, Johnny mentioned to me that he was having trouble during the race because of all the people who come out of the crowds to touch him or slap him on the back," says Donovan. "We have a pair of troopers now who protect Johnny along the way.

"Just before the race, all the elite runners seclude themselves in the basement of the First Congregational Church of Hopkinton. It's by invitation only. I remember we were having trouble getting through the barriers to the church. Johnny didn't want to wait for these big metal barriers to be moved, so he jumped over them."

In the church basement Johnny joined his two escorts, Trooper John Murphy and Sgt. Bill Coulter, a triathlete who had also protected Johnny the year before. "He's one of my idols," says Coulter. "The day of the Marathon, he's a different person; he's extremely focused.

"We really are his bodyguards during the race. John Murphy and I are both about 6 feet tall, 180 pounds, but we really take a body beating. At the start, 8,000 people are trying to run up Mr. Kelley's back, so we run shoulder-to-shoulder. Everyone is caught up in their own race, and some of them complain until they get around us and see Mr. Kelley."

"They're wonderful," Johnny says of his escorts. "They do a great job protecting me. Some drunk came at me saying, 'You're better than the Celtics.' They took care of him. They almost took care of my sister, too! She came out of the crowd and almost got her arm broken before I could tell them who she was."

Shooting for a five-hour finish, Johnny fell victim to the bitter cold and pelting rain that plagued him the last ten miles. "It started raining around Auburndale and it was miserable the rest of the way.

"When I was running up Heartbreak Hill, near Boston College, there were about fifty young people up there. They formed a narrow little lane for me to go through and they were chanting, 'Go, Johnny, go! Go, Johnny, go!'

"Somehow or another I kept going along and going along, and then after Boston College I said, 'Gee, I've come this far, it's only a few more miles to go.' So I stopped and walked quite a bit."

Watching the race on Commonwealth Avenue was David Taugher, one of Kel's several "adopted sons." Seeing that Johnny's gloves were completely soaked, Taugher raced off to find replacements. "I ran into two retail stores, but I didn't have any money with me," says Taugher, a five-time finisher at Boston. "Then I went into a Chinese laundry to try and get a pair of socks, but they just looked at me and shook their heads."

While Taugher's fiancée ran alongside Johnny and his state police escorts, David raced ahead of them to his own apartment and returned with two long white stockings that warmed Johnny's hands the final freezing mile. "As if running the Boston Marathon wasn't enough of a gauntlet in itself," says Taugher, "three or four heavy metal pipes fell off a passing truck and came rolling at us! I ran out ahead of Johnny and stopped them with my foot."

"It was wonderful to see David and Rita," says Johnny. "They kept talking to me and really kept me going. They pulled me through great. I said, 'Gee, I'm gonna make it! I'm gonna make it!' "

Johnny's sixtieth Boston was an ordeal and at several points along the way it looked like he might have been wiser to quit. But with Laura waiting, and a laurel wreath and special 60th B.A.A. banner beckoning, Johnny Kelley pressed on, unwilling to yield. When he at last reached Boylston Street, he was greeted by a group of loyal, loving fans who simply wouldn't go home without seeing Mr. Marathon reach the line. "I still can't believe those people stood in the rain and waited for me. It brings tears to my eyes."

Rejuvenated by the emotional welcome, Johnny thanked his two escorts and trotted home ahead of them. His time of 5:42:54 was by far his slowest. But time wasn't the point. What mattered was that a proud, persistent little white-haired man named Johnny Kelley, who has run this race through *eight decades,* had gone the distance again.

Five months after the most strenuous Marathon of his life, Johnny Kelley sits at his kitchen table recounting the trials and triumphs of his long, inspiring life. He has just celebrated another birthday. "I'm 84 years old," he says, hardly believing it himself. "Don't let this altar-boy face fool you."

The face won't fool a soul, but the way he fidgets in his chair does remind one of a restless adolescent anxious to be released from his lessons. In fact, it seems Johnny rarely sits for more than a minute or two. He appears to be always moving, always excited or occupied by something. How does Laura deal with this constant motion? "I go read a book," she says. "Actually one might think that John would be always talking and never stop. But during the evening he quite often sits on the sofa or stretches out for a nap or reads his magazines and is very quiet all evening. Nobody would believe it, but it's true. He wants to keep going all the time, go out and work around the property, but in spite of that, he's a restful person. I think of him as being quite peaceful."

"I had the fireplace inspected," Johnny says. "Next month we're gonna get a fire going. We love a fire. It's like having another person in the room. I like to have a Kelley cocktail (a glass of Chablis or a can of beer) by the fire now and then. Except for a Bloody Mary once in a while, I don't touch hard liquor. But I love a Chablis. I can't deny myself everything, after all."

"It's a wonderful life here," he says. "We have a lot of young friends that have adopted us."

One of Johnny's several "adopted sons" is Guy Morse, race director of the Boston Marathon, who also lives on Cape Cod. "I don't know if I've adopted him or he's adopted me, but Johnny bounces things off me quite a bit," says Morse, "We've grown very close.

"Last year, President Bush was on the Cape in Mashpee and we arranged for Johnny to meet him, and of course the President knew who Johnny was. On the way home, we were talking about the celebration of Johnny's sixtieth Boston Marathon, and he asked me if I thought maybe he should sing something other than "Young At Heart." He was worried people might be getting sick of it. All the way home from Mashpee he auditioned different songs for me.

"Johnny is so much a part of the fabric of this intricate tapestry we call the Boston Marathon," says Morse. "He is really the common thread. He embodies everything that is special and worth preserving about the race itself.

"We talked to Johnny before last year's race about having him start ten or fifteen minutes ahead of everyone else so he can get the attention he deserves. But to Johnny, getting a head start would be a little like cheating. He's still a competitor, and he doesn't want to be treated any different from the other runners."

If someone hints at any special arrangements that don't include running the Marathon from start to finish, Johnny's gaze turns to ice. It has been suggested to him that he just run half of the Marathon, fire the gun or ride in the pace car. "As long as I have the health and the desire and the cooperation of my wife, I want to run. People always ask me if I'm gonna run next year. It all depends. If I'm feeling alright, I'll run. If I can't make it and have to take a ride, nobody better say anything, not with my record."

Jerry Nason once wrote of Johnny, "In truth, should Kel show any signs of failure to reach his goal, the crowds would very probably pick him up and hand him on down the line to the finish like a bucket of water in a fire brigade."

"Johnny Kelley is as traditional as the Marathon itself," says old friend Will Cloney. "If he drops dead running, that would be O.K. with him. He's a heroic figure, a national treasure."

"I've had a good life," Johnny says. "If it gets any better, I think I'll bust. I have no regrets. I never knowingly hurt anybody and I've never been in the slammer. I represented my country in the war and two Olympics. God's been good to me. I hope my career goes on for a few more years before I go to runner's heaven. Running the Boston

Marathon with all those people cheering—it's better than my birthday!

"I didn't try to set this record, you know. It just happened. But if anyone ever does break my record, I'd love to shake his hand."

"You're an Inspiration"
by Don Kardong

We are nearing the top of Heartbreak Hill, the section of the Boston course named for the poor fellow who, in so many races in the 1930s and '40s, approached this point as the leader of the race, only to head down toward Cleveland Circle a few minutes later behind the winner: Johnny Kelley. And I'm right next to him.

I look at Kelley. He is not quite walking, because his arms are up and swinging. But he is not exactly running either, judging by the placement of his feet upon roadway. This, rather, is some sort of timeless, indefinable motion, an expression of human will overcoming entropy. Here in April 1991, we've been at this for more than 4 hours, 20 minutes, most recently at a clip of 15 minutes per mile, with rain falling steadily for a solid hour. Though chilled and wobbly, Mr. Marathon will not quit.

"Spectators, move to the side of the road," orders a police loudspeaker a few yards behind us, as it has for the past hour. "Traffic will be coming through."

Earlier, this section of the course had been packed with spectators. Patriots' Day celebrants who watched first Ibrahim Hussein, then Wanda Panfil, then another 10,000 runners race, run, and hobble by. By the time Kelley reaches Heartbreak, the crowd has thinned to three basic groups: 1) Race volunteers; 2) people who wouldn't think of leaving the course until Johnny Kelley passes, even if it means risking pneumonia; and 3) drunks.

A group of about 50 of the latter, in fact, has just run 100 yards with Kelley, chanting, "John-NEE, John-NEE, John-NEE . . . " in an act of encouragement that borders on harassment.

Through all of this, the 83-year-old, 131-pound, blue-eyed, white-haired elder statesman of the Boston Marathon just plugs along. Flanked by two Massachusetts State Troopers, he pretty much ignores the maelstrom that surrounds him.

Dressed in long-sleeved cotton shirt, John Hancock singlet, and blue shorts over lavender tights, Kelley is not quite color-coordinated. Function overrides fashion for the veteran, who wears his wife's stocking cap and a painter's cap on his head, a white scarf around his neck, and gloves on his hands, all in a determined bid to keep the wet wolves of a rainy April day at bay.

"You're looking good, John!" shouts a man from under his umbrella. "You're looking unbelievable."

And then Kelley passes, and I hear the man say quietly to his friend, "Oh, he looks bad."

And who wouldn't? Wet, weary, over an hour from the finish, and struggling up the same monster that used to frustrate his aspirations a half-century earlier. At 83 years of age, who would argue if he were to simply call it off? Instead, the opposite happens. Cresting the top of Heartbreak, Kelley's stride changes ever so slightly, a subtle yet distinct metamorphosis. He is, I decide, running again.

Working on his sixtieth Boston Marathon, fifty-six of which he has already finished, the determination still burns. Johnny Kelley is, by God, going to get through this thing. He is one Cool-Hand-Luke-of-a-Rocky-Balboa of an octogenarian, refusing to give up. For a second, Kelley's gaze glances off the spot on the road five feet in front of him where he keeps it focused, and he looks toward downtown Boston. After all these years, the finish line still beckons.

Sixty Bostons! Johnny Kelley first toed the Boston starting line in 1928, a race he failed to finish. After a three-year hiatus, he tried again in 1932, but DNF-ed again. In 1933, though, he completed the distance in 3:03:56, beginning a streak that would carry him to the finish line every year except two—1956 and

1968—for the next fifty-eight years. His efforts included two victories —1935 and 1945—and seven second-
place finishes.

Will anyone ever equal this record? To do so, a runner would have to start young, stay healthy, maintain
interest, avoid injuries, and outrun the Grim Reaper for
nearly a century.

How has Kelley managed to do this? Sitting in the
invited runners area a few hours earlier, I am mysti-
fied by the question. I am nursing a calf pull, and I
have the thing all analgesic-ed and bandaged. I keep
shaking and patting it, and can't avoid the notion that
the 83-year-old on the other side of the room, a man
twice my age, is in better condition to finish twenty-six
miles than I am. In interviews, Kelley seems as baffled
by his good fortune in avoiding injuries as most of us
are in why we can't.

In fact, Kelley's biggest problem this day has been
dealing with the onslaught of media attention. There's
no question he enjoys the limelight, but enough has
been enough.

"I'm just trying to keep an even keel and keep my
head above water," he says a few minutes before noon.
"It's going to be a relief to get into the race."

On the starting line, the B.A.A. has painted Kelley a
special spot, a circle three feet in diameter with a
shamrock and "60" in the center. Nearby, circles of
past years—59, 58, 57, 56—surround it in ever-dimin-
ishing clarity, like memories of yesterday's performances. Kelley, though, after an introduction to the
throng, settles in on the opposite side of the road, with
his two bipedal police escorts just behind. I tuck in
behind them, along with Colin Corkery, a 33-year-old
runner who has agreed to shadow Kelley for a local TV
station.

At high noon, we're off. The elite runners whoosh by
on our right, and Johnny Kelley begins his mile-by-mile
trek to Boylston Street.

Mile 1—We are in the midst of a quest to keep faster runners from knocking Kelley over.

State Troopers John Murphy and William Coulter manage the task of directing human traffic around him with great skill and diplomacy. When people squeeze by, they seem irritated at first, but then, noticing Johnny, often shout, "Awright, Johnny!" We pass the mile mark in 10:10. Kelley will hold a pace of 10-12 minutes per mile for over half the race.

Mile 2—"There's Johnny Kelley!" shouts a spectator.

"Where?"

"Right there."

"Where?"

"Right there."

"Good luck, Mr. Kelley!"

Mile 3—We pass the first-aid station, and a chaotic scramble for fluids ensues. The troopers have their hands full trying to keep their charge from being trampled like a paper cup. About this same time, a discarded garbage bag gets caught in Kelley's feet, and he nearly tumbles.

A minute later, a woman leans from the side of the road to within inches of his face and shouts, "Attaboy, Johnny Kelley Sweetheart!"

Mile 4—A man bending over his young son says, "That's the man. That's the 83-year-old man, Johnny Kelley."

Mile 5—The second water stop seems a little safer, now that fewer runners are angling to get by. Kelley takes water, spits it out, and throws some over his head. We pass 5 miles in 51:49.

Mile 6—In the town of Framingham, a runner dressed as Groucho Marx goes by, turns, flicks a cigar and says, "Hey, Johnny, tell 'em Groucho sent you."

This and other acts that cry out for response go totally without comment by Kelley, whose gaze remains fixed on a spot five feet ahead. For a guy who is known to ham it up at the least provocation with a rendition of "Young at Heart," he takes today's task very seriously, ignoring runners and spectators alike. He must hear his name 10,000 times before the finish.

"Attaboy, Johnny!"

Just before the Framingham train station, a man passes by, pushing a canoe on wheels, with two kids in front. I hear him explaining about the old man in lavender tights.

Mile 7—Spectators run along the side of the road, then set up to take still pictures and video of the man of the hour.

"How to go, Johnny!"

Mile 8—We head up a hill, and I can sense him slowing down. For the first time, I wonder if he's going to make it.

Mile 9—As we pass a reservoir, the crowd suddenly gets quiet. Colin Corkery, who is running with a mobile phone next to me, reports that Hussein and Panfil are leading the race. Kelley continues to chug along.

Mile 10—Spectators call out, "We love you, Johnny!" and "You're an inspiration to us all, Johnny!"

Two runners pass, and I hear one say, "That's Johnny Kelley."

"Yeah," the other responds. "I understand he has an escort with him so idiots like us can't go up and say hello."

Mile 11—A woman yells, "Way to go, John Hancock." Both troopers laugh. There aren't many on this course who would get the sponsor singlet confused with the man who wears it.

Mile 12—"He's a marvelous person," enthuses a middle-aged woman at an impromptu aid station. "I can't believe he's running. Eighty-three years old! I'm thrilled that he took our water."

Mile 13—"I feel good!" shouts a man behind us, James Brown-style. "I knew that I would." His enthusiasm is wonderful, but nothing to match that of the women of Wellesley, who whoop and scream like

Arsenio Hall's studio audience upon learning that Tom Cruise is backstage. If this doesn't send the 83-year-old into some kind of ecstatic time warp, nothing will.

Mile 14—We pass halfway in 2:25:49, and Kelley seems oblivious to the rock 'n roll applause that greets him in the town of Wellesley. A runner jogs in front, pestering him with questions, until Kelley finally has to shout, "Get outta here!"

"Isn't he precious?" says one old lady. "He's just precious."

Precious and fragile and tired, and just over halfway.

Mile 15—"Kell-EE! Kell-EE! Kell-EE!" chants a group of about 50 revelers near the end of Wellesley.

Mile 16—The first sag wagons, yellow school buses with marathon drop-outs on board, pass. We feel sprinkles of rain.

A man who must be 60 years old sees Kelley go by, picks up his metal crutches, bangs them together, and shouts, "Go, Johnny!"

Mile 17—Going uphill out of Newton Lower Falls and passing over Interstate 95, Kelley's arms seem to drop. He looks tired, and I wonder if this is normal.

A man standing near an on-ramp leans out and asks if he needs anything. This is Dan Kelley, Johnny's nephew, who tells me that Johnny's grandfather came to the United States on a ship called the *S.S. Marathon*. He also admits that his uncle seems to be having a hard time.

"I've never seen him look that bad before," he says, speculating that the cold is getting to him. Shortly afterward, it starts to rain.

Mile 18—"C'mon, hang in there!" yells a spectator. Is it my imagination, or are his fans starting to look worried? By the time we turn onto Commonwealth Avenue, the rain is pouring down. Over two hours to go!

Mile 19—"Oooh, he doesn't look too happy," I hear from underneath an umbrella.

Mile 20—The crowds are thin now, though people occasionally rush from their houses when they realize Kelley is passing. Another sag wagon pulls next to us, and the driver asks Colin and me if we'd like to hop on.

And then, finally, Kelley reaches the top of his old nemesis, Heartbreak. His stride changes slightly, his determination redoubles, and he begins the shuffle through miles 22, 23, 24, and 25, among ever-increasing cheers.

"Don't let those troopers slow you down, Johnny!" shouts a spectator near Boston College.

"Way to go, Johnny!" yells a motorist. "You're an institution!" shouts a heavy-set man who jogs in front of Kelley for a hundred yards before being waved to the side. "You're better than the Celtics!"

"We love you, Johnny! You're an inspiration to us all!"

With just over a mile to go, we see a truck passing in the opposite direction which appears to hit three eight-foot metal pipes, which come careening toward Kelley. For a moment, it looks as if he might end his 60th Boston a mile from the finish, bowled over like a duckpin. But, with his escorts' help, he scoots away safely.

"You've got it now!" shouts a man from the third story of a nearby brownstone. "Less than a mile to go!"

Kelley's nose is turning purple, there are bags under his eyes, but he is finally allowing a smile to light his face. He knows he's going to make it. As we pass the Eliot Lounge, bartender Tommy Leonard greets Kelley with a red nose of his own.

After turning onto Hereford Street and then Boylston for the final straightaway, Kelley grabs the hands of his police escorts. Coulter and Murphy, thanks them, and then turns into the Johnny Kelley I've always seen in race photos.

Smiling, waving and giving a thumbs up, he travels the final quarter-mile to the finish, while sirens whoop-whoop-whoop, people shout encouragement from buildings along the way, and spectators jump up and down on the sidewalks next to him, taking time from picture-taking to give one more "All right, Johnny!" yell.

As the clock reaches 5:42:54, Johnny Kelley the Elder, the man they describe as the heart and soul of the Boston marathon, who twice in his life has crossed this line before anyone else, finishes again.

A minute later, race officials push away the man who has completed his 57th Boston Marathon in a wheelchair. After nearly six hours on his feet, he deserves a ride.

I don't know if Johnny Kelley will attempt another Boston. When I asked him before the race, he just said, "I hope so."

Some day, of course, he'll be done traveling from Hopkinton to Boston on foot, and the chants of "John-NEE! John-NEE! John-NEE!" at the back of the Boston pack will be history, replaced by something else.

But it's hard to imagine another runner replacing Johnny Kelley, surviving enough Patriots' Days to challenge his record.

Perhaps one day it will happen. Decades from now, someone may have a shot at it, and spectators will line the course as they do every year at Boston to watch. There will be buds on the branches in Wellesley, and daffodils and azalea bushes in bloom. And some man standing alongside the road, cheering this future phenomenon, may remember a day in April 1991, when he stood as a child and watched an 83-year-old man set the standard.

And he will remember his father, turning to him and saying, "See that man there. He's 83 years old."

And he will remember asking, "What's his name, Dad?"

And the name will come drifting back in memory, timeless, "Johnny Kelley."

Don Kardong finished 4th in the 1976 Olympic marathon in 2 hours, 11 minutes and 16 seconds. His 1991 Boston Marathon journey with Johnny Kelley took a bit longer than that. A senior writer for *Runner's World* magazine, Kardong is the author of *Thirty Phone Booths to Boston* and *Hills, Hawgs and Ho Chi Minh*.

EPILOGUE

In 1992 Johnny Kelley once again perambulated from Hopkinton to Boston on Patriots' Day. The previous year had been marred by wind-driven rain and a nasty fall after crossing the finish line. This time, the sky was clear and there were still hundreds of spectators in the grandstands when Johnny reached the line in just under 6 hours. One of those admirers waiting to pay tribute was Ibrahim Hussein of Kenya who had won the race 4 hours earlier. Hussein proclaimed Kelley "the greatest runner of us all."

"I've never had any of the winners ever do that before," Kelley told reporters.

Less than a week later, Johnny announced his retirement. "I've been thinking about it since last year," he told Larry Ames of the *Boston Globe*. "But I didn't finish well last year. It was raining and I fell down, and I didn't want to end it that way. This year I think I went out with a bang."

Among the many who have been inspired by Johnny's longevity was Dr. Wayman Spence of Waco, Texas. The good doctor decided to commemorate Kel's career by commissioning a statue that now stands at the foot of Heartbreak Hill near Newton City Hall. On April 18, a glorious Sunday afternoon before the 97th running of the BAA, Johnny unveiled the 7-foot sculpture, which is in fact a dual portrait of the Marathon's patron saint. On the left is a likeness of

Kelley at age 27 when he first won Boston in 1935. The statue on the right depicts the octogenarian crowd pleaser of later years, waving his cap to the crowd. The two Kelleys are linked, hand in hand, as they cross the finish line together. "This statue tops everything. I'm full of love today for everybody," Johnny declared, before treating the crowd to a rousing rendition of "Young at Heart."

Joining the 600 or so who attended the ceremony was four-time winner Bill Rodgers. "Johnny epitomizes the marathon race itself," Rodgers told the crowd. "I mean this isn't golf. You have to really endure in this sport."

For the next two years the sculpture served as Johnny's starting line. Once again Troopers Bill Coulter and John Murphy were Kelley's escorts. After nearly 20 miles of running, they reached the foot of Heartbreak Hill where Johnny joined them for his own 6.6-mile jaunt to the finish, applause accompanying every step.

In March of 1995, after a debilitating stroke, Laura, Johnny's wife of nearly 40 years, passed away at age 84. Still rising before the sun, Johnny's morning runs, now actually more of a steady shuffle, helped him cope with the grief. "It's the laughs I miss the most," he told the Boston Herald. "We used to joke around a lot."

Knowing that Johnny was now living a lonely existence on Cape Cod, staving off both age and sadness, B.A.A. officials suggested that he stop running and serve as grand marshal. Johnny accepted the proposal. "I'm going to be a big shot. I'll be up front riding in a big red convertible. No heavy lifting. I hope it doesn't rain."

When Kelley climbed up on the back seat of the fire engine-red Trans Am to prepare for his ride from Hopkinton Green to Copley Square, race volunteers got nervous. "Don't worry," Johnny said, "I won't fall off." He enjoyed his new role immensely, waving to the cheering throngs. "The crowds have been so supportive, I think I'm going to run for governor." He also enjoyed seeing men's winner Cosmos Ndeti cross the finish line. "It was the first finish I've seen since 1945."

Though it seemed that Johnny Kelley had been honored in every manner possible, the next few years brought even more accolades. In 1996, he was awarded a Doctor of Humane Letters degree from Boston University. In 1999, the editors of *Runner's World* magazine named John A. Kelley, then 92, Runner of the Century. "By far, in our opinion, it is the greatest running achievement of the century. The years and times alone can't give full measure to his legacy. His energy, persistence and excellence have inspired untold millions of runners worldwide."

"I just can't believe it," Kelley exclaimed. "It's the highest honor I've ever received."

Being named Runner of the Century ended a low year on a high note. In January 1999, he underwent emergency abdominal surgery to repair a perforation in his colon. A subsequent bout with pneumonia set back his recovery. But a long lifetime of rigorous training helped him get through the ordeal. By early April he was returning to his old spry self. Still, not wanting to risk a recurrence of pneumonia, Old Kel was not in Boston on Patriots' Day for the first time in 67 years. At a press conference announcing his decision, Johnny chuckled. "I'm finally learning patience," he said, thinking back once again to the impulsiveness that probably cost him two or three more victories at Boston during his prime.

There in spirit, Johnny sent a tape recording of himself singing "Young at Heart," which was played at the champions' breakfast two days before the race. Johnny watched the 103rd running on television from his room at a rehab center in Harwich. Seated next to him was Ginger DeLong, who had become his loving companion. In 2002 Johnny, at age 95, married Ginger, 78.

With his new wife by his side, Johnny resumed his regular routine of appearances at road races and charitable events, looking fit and always sounding upbeat. He would occasionally mention an uncle who lived to be 101. "I'd like to live that long," he said, setting yet another goal. But while breakfasting at the Marshside, a favorite restaurant near his home, Johnny uttered a seemingly prophetic statement to his nephew, Tom. "I have no regrets," he told me. "I lived a good life." On October 6, precisely one month after his 97th birthday, just hours after being moved to a rehabilitation center near his home, Johnny Kelley passed away.

"I dreaded getting this news," B.A.A. race director Guy Morse told the *Cape Cod Times*. "In some ways I never thought it would happen. I guess I wanted Johnny to be forever."

Though he barely missed seeing his beloved Boston Red Sox end 86 years of heartache by finally winning the World Series, Johnny

Kelley missed little else in life. At his funeral Mass, his stepson, David DeLong, told the more than 300 mourners, "He was a man who always marveled at the blessings of his health, his friends, and all the love he felt from his many admirers, and I think that's one of the things that kept him young at heart so long—all the affection."

In spirit, Johnny Kelley will never really stop running the Boston Marathon. He will traverse the meandering route from Hopkinton to Boston forever, bounding up and over Heartbreak Hill, hurrying down Commonwealth Avenue, waving to the delighted crowds, thanking them for all their love.

Johnny Kelley's Boston Marathon Record

YEAR	AGE	TIME	FINISH
1928	20	DNF	—
1932	24	DNF	—
1933	25	3:03:56	37
1934	26	2:36:50	2
1935	27	2:32:07	1
1936	28	2:38:49	5
1937	29	2:39:02	2
1938	30	2:37:34	3
1939	31	2:41:03	13
1940	32	2:32:03	2
1941	33	2:31:26	2
1942	34	2:37:55	5
1943	35	2:30:00	2
1944	36	2:32:03	2
1945	37	2:30:40	1
1946	38	2:31:27	2
1947	39	2:40:00	13
1948	40	2:37:50	4*
1949	41	2:38:07	4*
1950	42	2:43:45	5*
1951	43	2:39:09	6*
1952	44	3:04:59	12
1953	45	2:32:46	7*
1954	46	2:50:25	16
1955	47	2:45:22	24
1956	48	DNF	—
1957	49	2:53:00	13
1958	50	2:52:12	9*
1959	51	2:47:52	23
1960	52	2:44:39	19
1961	53	2:44:53	17
1962	54	2:44:36	25

YEAR	AGE	TIME	FINISH
1963	55	3:14:00	84
1964	56	2:49:14	48
1965	57	2:48:00	58
1966	58	2:55:00	59
1967	59	3:13:00	135
1968	60	DNS	—
1969	61	3:05:02	186**
1970	62	3:03:00	163**
1971	63	3:45:47	977
1972	64	3:35:12	890
1973	65	3:35:02	1,105
1974	66	3:24:10	1,266
1975	67	3:22:48	1,633
1976	68	3:28:00	1,094
1977	69	3:32:12	1,892
1978	70	3:42:36	3,729
1979	71	3:45:12	NA
1980	72	3:35:21	3,444
1981	73	4:01:25	5,074
1982	74	4:01:30	NA
1983	75	4:23:22	NA
1984	76	sub-5:00	NA
1985	77	4:31:00	NA
1986	78	4:27:00	NA
1987	79	4:19:56	NA
1988	80	4:26:36	NA
1989	81	5:05:15	NA
1990	82	5:05:00	NA
1991	83	5:42:54	NA
1992	84	5:58:36	NA

DNF—Did not finish
DNS—Did not start
*Number 1 master (40 and over)
**Number 1 senior (60 and over)
NA—Not Available